"This is a book I have been have done a beautiful job (and isn't!), showing how it might look like in actio sial and potentially divisive think this will be so helpful in all kinds of contexts as together we work out what biblical faithfulness looks like in the life of the local church and beyond."

Gary Millar, Principal, Queensland Theological College, Australia

"Here's a book for those looking for sound reasoning and humble guidance in regard to the practical application of complementarity in a variety of church contexts. Graham and Jane graciously and consistently apply what the Scriptures teach with a lack of rigidity yet with firm conviction in regard to the biblical call for men and women to express their godliness through gender."

Nancy Guthrie, Author; Bible Teacher

"I much enjoyed reading this fresh, sensitive, thoughtful, well-informed and engagingly positive treatment of what is so often seen as just a troublesome and controversial topic. The authors leave space for readers to come to different conclusions in detail, under the shelter of a glad affirmation of the goodness of the word of God in every passage of Scripture. I especially valued the tone of gentle gladness allied to a confident affirmation of essentials."

Christopher Ash, Writer-in-Residence, Tyndale House, Cambridge

"This helpful book will challenge you to think through the implications of your complementarian convictions and then put them into practice at your church. Every local church should consult it."

Colleen McFadden, Director of Women's Workshops, Charles Simeon Trust

"Writing a book on complementarianism today is like lighting a match in the dry forest of Western society. It can ignite a raging controversy in a culture deeply conflicted about gender. But Jane Tooher and Graham Beynon commend complementarianism in a clear, and compelling way. Their book is biblically rich and wisely applied for God's people as his beautiful design."

Richard Chin, National Director, Australian Fellowship of Evangelical Students; Author, *Captivated by Christ* and *How to Read the Bible Better*

"This outstanding book is deeply grounded in the Bible, shows a clear grasp of the contexts in which our churches are working, and is thoroughly readable and highly stimulating. It will help you rethink your convictions. It will encourage you to value highly the ministries of women and men. It will challenge you to work out together what you believe about women's ministry in the life of the church. It will provide excellent pathways towards implementation of positive complementary ministry."

William Taylor, Rector, St Helen's Bishopsgate, London, UK

"This is a brilliant book to help church leadership teams think through how they implement complementarian convictions. The authors are enormously sympathetic to the wide variety of personal and church experiences which readers will bring to these questions. They helpfully challenge whether complementarian churches actually embody equality and whether they manifest a genuine feel of family, rather than just asserting those things. Whatever your personal convictions on the relevant biblical texts, Graham and Jane ask really helpful questions to make sure that these convictions are lived out in a manner which produces a mutual flourishing of the sexes."

Matt Fuller, Senior Pastor, Christ Church Mayfair, London, UK;
Author, *Be True to Yourself*

"A really useful book. It clearly explains the various positions on complementarianism and the potential imbalances that each is prone to. You will be equipped to examine and understand your own position and to embrace it with clarity, conviction and joy."

Jennie Pollock, Author, *If Only: Finding Joyful Contentment in the Face of Lack and Longing*

"Those of us who believe the Bible teaches distinct roles for men and women in church cannot presume to commend our view on the strength of our exegesis alone. We need urgently to show not only that it is true but that it is good. We need to be able to point to healthy local churches and ministries and say, 'There! Like that! That's how it's done well.' Tooher and Beynon have written a book that speaks directly and compellingly to this need. It's a book that moves beyond the 'what' to the 'how.' Both authors have extensive ministry experience, which shines through in their writing. They understand that for most of us, the challenge is not so much what the Bible says but how to land it faithfully and fruitfully in the actual circumstances of mission and ministry in the 21st century."

Rory Shiner, Senior Pastor, Providence Church,
Perth, Western Australia; Author

"We always need to teach the truth about what the Lord says, confident that it will be a blessing. This fine book gives us the courage to see that the complementarian position is good for us as we experience what it is like to belong to the family of God. It shows that as we truly model family in the church, we will be witnessing to the world around us about the transforming power of the gospel. Read it and see."

Peter Jensen, Former Archbishop of Sydney

"There are many superb books on the theology of complementarianism, but this one is different! It gives complementarianism 'legs' and probes what it could look like on the ground in your local church. The emphasis is on exploring ways for men and women to minister together rather than settling for the status quo. I've worked at the coalface of complementarianism for 30 years, but my intuition tells me that this book has the potential to transform the complementary ministry of men and women for a new generation."

Lesley Ramsay, Evangelist; Trainer; Bible Teacher

"In a day when polemics are often wielded on both the right and the left, it is refreshing to read an irenic and immensely practical book on what it means to embrace complementarianism. Beynon and Tooher's book will help pastors and church leaders (and laypeople too!) to think carefully about what it means to include both men and women in the ministry of the church in a complementarian framework. I hope this book will be read widely and will lead to further clarity, understanding and humility as we work out what it means for both men and women to be involved in the ministry of the church."

Thomas R. Schreiner, James Buchanan Harrison Professor of New Testament Interpretation, The Southern Baptist Theological Seminary

"*Embracing Complementarianism* paints an engaging and persuasive picture of what complementarianism might look like in the local church. It is neither dismissive of alternative views nor prescriptive of the conclusions reached by the authors. Rather, it raises some vitally important questions about men and women serving together in ministry, and encourages pastors and churches to reflect deeply on their convictions about Scripture's teaching in this area, and the way they are, or are not, put into practice. It's a book to make use of, not merely to read and keep on the shelf. This is the book on complementarianism we've been waiting for!"

Kanishka Raffel, Archbishop of Sydney

"The abuse of power by some prominent church leaders in recent years has left many in our constituency wondering if the complementarian position is as toxic as some would suggest. Certainly, those who define complementarianism purely on the basis of what women cannot do are shooting themselves in the foot and exposing their ignorance. So, what does it mean to be complementarian, and how can we be sure that our biblical convictions are having a positive rather than a negative impact on our church culture? In this book, Graham and Jane are not just asking us to consider the biblical principles but actually show us (and model for us) what it means to embrace them and live by them. If we believe that God's design for men and women is for our good, then embracing it is not an optional extra for Christians but absolutely key if our families and churches are to flourish."

Carrie Sandom, Director of Women's Ministry,
The Proclamation Trust, London

"Here is a fresh and envisioning guide to help church leaders move beyond an embarrassed defence of complementarianism to advancing a positive vision of men and women working together in a local church."

Paul Rees, Lead Pastor of Charlotte Chapel, Edinburgh, Scotland

"Few issues have generated more controversy in our culture and the church in recent years than the relationship between men and women. Complementarian theology has been condemned by some as abusive, and its advocates have all too often taken a defensive approach. Drawing on their many years of church ministry and training experience in Britain and Australia, the authors present a compelling, positive vision for complementarianism that rejects outdated stereotypes in favour of a holistic biblical vision of God's creational plan for men and women. Irenic in tone, culturally sensitive and exegetically rooted, this book will help reluctant complementarians to more joyfully embrace what they believe. Egalitarians evangelicals who read it will gain a better understanding of the convictions and concerns of complementarian brothers and sisters. It unpacks the practical implications of complementarianism for church life without being prescriptive and provides helpful reflection questions for individuals and groups."

John Stevens, National Director,
Fellowship of Independent Evangelical Churches, UK

EMBRACING
COMPLEMENTARIANISM

Graham Beynon and Jane Tooher

Embracing Complementarianism
© Graham Beynon and Jane Tooher, 2022.
Reprinted 2023

Published by The Good Book Company

thegoodbook.com | thegoodbook.co.uk
thegoodbook.com.au | thegoodbook.co.nz | thegoodbook.co.in

Cover design by Faceout Studio | Art direction and design by André Parker

ISBN: 9781784987671 | Printed in Turkey

Contents

From Graham:
To Fiona Hamilton, Paula Harris, Jo Scoones, Fiona Doel, and Jo Thomson, who I've been privileged to work with.

From Jane:
To Phillip Jensen, Phil Wheeler, Marcus Nodder, John Woodhouse, and Mark Thompson. Good bosses, and great co-workers in the Lord.

1.
Complementarianism Today

When we've shared that we're writing a book about embracing complementarianism, we've been met with a variety of responses. Some people say, "Oh good! Something on this at last". But most people say, "Oh dear! That's going to be difficult".

Teaching about complementarianism often is. The last time Graham spoke on this at his church, the ripples started in the question time following the sermon, then continued into lunch following the service, and carried on for months. No one was acting badly, and the questions and discussions were all good and worthwhile—but there were lots of them. Talking about gender raises issues that can be awkward, controversial, and hard to navigate. No wonder many people think that it's a subject best avoided—why stir up a hornet's nest?

EMBARRASSED COMPLEMENTARIANISM?

Simply put, complementarianism is the belief that God made men and women equal and distinctive: equal in value and dignity, and distinctive in certain responsibilities and roles. It is a conviction which has historically been the normal position and practice of the church across the world, but which, in recent decades, has become a storm centre.

Some of that debate comes from changes in our wider society which have pressured and challenged the church. Issues of gender swirl around in our culture with alarming ferocity, and they connect to deeply held feelings about equality and justice. Saying that men and women are different, and that they might have different roles, has been out of step with most of Western culture for a long time. To say that a woman is not *allowed* to do something because she's a woman is baffling, to say the least. And, many in our culture would now consider the notion of "gender roles" to be not only weird but also morally wrong and potentially damaging to both women and men.

How you respond to such social change will depend on a number of factors, not least your own background. You might have accepted "traditional" roles for women and men without really thinking it through, because that has been your experience, or it is attractive to you and it seems to offer definite structures and security. If so, you'll probably feel disturbed by these cultural waves. You might respond by fighting back or suddenly wondering if you're a cultural dinosaur. Or, conversely, you might feel a resonance with our culture; perhaps you are worried or angry that the church really is perpetuating authoritarian male leadership and sexism, which at best limits women's gifting and at worst harms people. In which case, you will want to push for change.

But debate and angst do not just come from interactions with the surrounding culture; they are generated within the church as well. We want to please and honour God, but that means knowing God's will for a situation. So, understandably, we ask, "What does complementarianism look like?" or "What should women do or not do?" We might worry that we've mistaken traditionalism for right biblical understanding. Or we might see that the Bible teaches a complementarian position but feel uncomfortable or embarrassed about it. Deep down, we'd really prefer that it didn't say such things.

None of that is helped by the growing divergence within the complementarian camp. There are several different possible positions on the roles of men and women, which can be confusing to navigate—and if their proponents are confident, and even strident, they easily cause worry and potential guilt for those who think they disagree.

Then we can add the track record of churches and the personal histories of individuals. Many women *have* been limited in what they can do in church life—and that might have been done for good or bad reasons, and might have been done lovingly, blindly or harshly. Some women have been treated appallingly, while others haven't but perceive that they have. Some will think their gifts have been slighted and the church weakened by limitation of their ministry, and they might be right. But our point for now is that none of us can pretend to come to this "cold". We all have history of some sort. Sometimes that history is good and affirming; unfortunately, often it isn't. And each of us then brings our responses to that history to the table too. Church leaders must recognise that while complementarianism could be thought of as a relatively minor issue in church order, it has affected some people's relationship with church and their faith as a whole.

Given all this, it's not surprising that some in the church respond by ducking the issue: they stick with familiar patterns of church and ministry and in effect say, "Let's not rock the boat". They might add that there are more important things to get on with ("There's a world that needs to hear the gospel") and so we should leave contentious issues to one side. This might include comments about it being a "secondary issue" and "agreeing to disagree". While there can be wisdom in such responses, and we will return to some of these elements, at worst this is simply sweeping it under the carpet. If

God has spoken about gender—and if he always speaks what is right and true, and if his ways are always good and freeing for us—then we ignore what he says at our peril.

EMBRACING COMPLEMENTARIANISM

Imagine being part of a church that wasn't confused, or reluctant, or reticent about complementarianism—but rather *embraced* it. Imagine being so convinced of what God says that you're able to express it confidently in what you say and do. Imagine being so compelled by the goodness of what God says that you express it positively in church life. Imagine if God's design for men and women wasn't something you were reluctant to accept or a little bit embarrassed about—but something you delighted in. And if you're thinking, "I can't imagine that I would ever feel like that (let alone other people in my church)", then we believe this book can help you. It's written primarily for people in church leadership—elders, staff members, church councils or leadership boards and so on—but not exclusively so. We hope that any engaged church member will find it helpful, although we acknowledge that some of its applications can only be implemented by a church's leaders.

Our conviction is that teaching and practising a more robust complementarianism leads people from a reluctant acceptance to a joyful embracing of God's word in this area. There are many books available which examine the biblical evidence for complementarianism and the arguments for and against. By and large, they do that well—but it is usually done from a position of trying to *defend* the complementarian position. While we will inevitably rehearse some of the same areas, we instead want to *advance* the complementarian position—to explore it and discuss it from the inside, as it were—and so help you embrace it.

So this book will try to do a few things differently to many others. We want to go *wider*—wider than the usual discussion of contested passages and arguments that establish the complementarian position. While these have their place, we also need to consider wider issues such as gender itself, the nature of church, and the components of ministry. You can think of these as bigger pieces of a jigsaw puzzle into which complementarianism fits. But they aren't often discussed very much, or even at all.

We also want to go *deeper*: deeper into what "equal and distinctive" means in practice; deeper into how the issues of equality and distinctiveness are fleshed out in real church life; and deeper into the different practical decisions that have to be made. As a result, this book will basically assume a complementarian position rather than argue for one, although we will look at some of the key passages on the way through.

We also want to be *positive*. Much talk around complementarianism can be negative in tone, only really emphasising what women cannot do. At other times, the discussion is tinged with embarrassment about placing any limit on the role of women, and so it emphasises that limits only apply to a few areas of church life and moves quickly on. We want to strike a different tone: to embrace complementarianism as God's good design and spend some time exploring what it looks like.

CONCERNS WITH COMPLEMENTARIANISM TODAY

Let's begin by thinking about where complementarian churches are typically starting from. Here are four concerns we have about how complementarianism can often end up looking in churches in the West today. The danger of this type of general critique is that it may well not be true of you or your church, at least in its entirety. But we do believe that these are significant issues in a great many complementarian churches today, and so it is helpful to identify them.

Separatism

The first concern is separatism: that is, that women's ministry tends to get separated from other, general ministry. So, you end up with "normal ministry" for everyone, such as preaching and small-group Bible studies—and then there's women's ministry, which often involves a women's Bible-study group, one-to-one discipleship, counselling, toddler groups and so on. There is undoubtedly lots of great ministry happening in these settings, and there are sometimes male equivalents. There can also be lots of logistical reasons as to why things get organised like this, and even some advantages in having separate streams.

Our concern, though, is that if ministries become mainly separate, there isn't much complementing going on. While you won't find the word "complementarian" in the Bible (it's been chosen to sum up a position), it nonetheless captures a dynamic that's woven throughout Scripture—of men and women *complementing* each other: a synergy that comes through togetherness. If a church has mainly separate ministries, though, it can be hard to see how the contributions of men and women combine to give an outcome that is greater than the sum of its parts.

Focus on boundaries

The second concern is that complementarianism leads to a focus on boundaries. The question becomes: What can a woman do or not do? Where are the boundaries lines? Can a woman lead a mixed-sex Bible study, teach teenage children, lead the whole congregation in prayer, lead a Sunday service or preach a sermon? Of course, we have to answer questions like these because we have to make decisions about what will happen in practice. The concern isn't that those decisions get made; the concern is that the ministry of women sometimes then becomes all about *staying inside the permitted boundaries.*

In any area of the Christian life, if behaviour is reduced to a series of "yes/no" answers, the chances are that we've missed something of the dynamic that should be in play. Decisions in Christian life and ministry are rarely check-box answers. One author, Michelle Lee-Barnewall, draws a parallel with ethical questions.[1] Imagine, she says, if someone asked if they could drink alcohol or gamble as a Christian. It's not a wrong question, and we would have to help them answer it so that they could decide how to live. But if our approach was to only give "yes/no" answers to those sorts of questions, we'd be missing something. We'd be missing a bigger perspective on what a holy life is all about, how sanctification works, and how it flows from the gospel.

Questions and answers that focus on boundaries usually miss the dynamics that shape the actual decision made. In a similar way, a focus on who can do what in church is likely to miss the beauty of the relational dynamics between men and women. Sadly, that's the flavour of much complementarianism today.

De-contextualisation

The third concern is that much of the discussion of complementarianism in church life and ministry is de-contextualised. All ministry takes place in the context of churches, and our understanding of what a church *is* should shape everything that happens within them. Such an understanding of church includes its identity, the nature of Christian relationships, ministry and gifting, and much more. But a broader discussion of this kind of ecclesiology, and how it shapes complementarianism, rarely appears.

We can draw a helpful parallel with marriage. Here, too, there's the question of what headship and submission mean and what they look like in practice. But the context for that discussion is our understanding of marriage more broadly. Headship and submission will look very different if you think of marriage primarily as voluntary cohabitation or as an economic transaction, compared to viewing it as a union where husband and wife become "one flesh" (Genesis 2:24). They would certainly *feel* very different. So with church life, our understanding of the wider context of church shapes not only what happens but how it happens and what it feels like.

Individualism

Our last concern is individualism. In Western culture there is a deep prevalence of individualistic thought, and we need to be alert as to how that influences our thinking on this issue. One study analysed which countries were the most individualistic in their outlook. Which do you think were the top three? It was the USA, Australia, and the United Kingdom. In these three countries, more than anywhere else in the world, we tend towards individualistic rather than communal thought; we instinctively think of ourselves as an individual, "I", rather than as a group, "we".

We are usually unaware of this because it is simply the air we breathe. When we grow up in a society, we adopt its way of thinking without thinking! But that way of thinking about ourselves and the world then acts as a lens through which we view everything, including the issue of complementarianism. Within individualistic societies the questions get shaped in a certain way: "who am I, and what can I do?" The answers I get to these questions are then key to my identity and sense of fulfilment.

This relates to our society's trend towards what has been called "expressive individualism", where our identity is achieved by expressing who we are. Such an outlook will inevitably lean towards concluding that I must be able to do certain things to express who God has made me. It is good and right to ask how God has made me and what contribution I can make. However, we should realise that how we approach these questions, and how we respond to them, risks being shaped more by the priorities of our individualistic culture than by the priorities of the Bible.

The biblical picture of humanity is that we were not made to live as individuals. Yes, we have an individual identity—but we're designed to live in community. God himself exists as a community of three Persons—Father, Son, and Holy Spirit—and he made us in his image. Moreover, God's plan of salvation is not to save individuals but to create a people for himself who reflect him in the way they live together. It is only in community that we truly know ourselves and flourish as the people God has made us.

Our concern then is that individualism has had a significant effect on how we think of ourselves and our ministries, and so has shaped our discussions and decisions around complementarianism. That needs to be challenged and examined; and that's what we hope to start to do.

HOW WE APPROACH COMPLEMENTARIANISM

Before we go any further, we need to outline the assumptions underlying our approach. This is key in any dialogue—if we have different approaches, we'll end up in different places. Here are four truths that will function as guiding principles in tackling the issues involved.

1. We accept God's word as good, right and authoritative

Since the Bible is God's word (not Graham's or Jane's), it reflects his character. This is excellent news for us! God is completely holy, infinitely loving, utterly good and entirely sovereign. Therefore, what God says in his word about us is *always* right, and it is *always* for our good. It comes to us from one who is not sinful; he knows and wants what is best for us; he is able to give us what we need; and he has met our greatest need when, through Jesus Christ's death and resurrection, he dealt with our sins for ever. The word of such a God is definitely good for us! This means we can confidently accept God's word as the final authority in all things, including on the subject of men and women. Any other authority we have—such as human reason, traditions or our experience—needs to be secondary to what God says in the Bible.

When we understand that God's word is good, right and authoritative in what it says about men and women, it helps us to:

(i)   fully embrace what God says positively and without embarrassment.

(ii)   not be legalistic in applying what he says within our churches.

(iii) recognise the authority of God's word over all people for all time, and so to bow to him rather than our culture.

That leads us to our next principle.

2. We read and apply the Bible within our own culture

We do not read the Bible in a vacuum. We all read it from within a location in time and space and as part of a specific group of people. 21st-century Western culture has been shaped not only by the Bible but also by rationalism, modern science, anti-institutionalism, feminism, secularism and much more. In each of these there is a combination of both good and bad. When we are reading or explaining the Bible, it is always worth asking ourselves how much of what we are saying is actually from the Bible, and how much is coming from the cultural framework we are bringing to it.

The first step is to recognise that because we are naturally sinful, we all have a tendency to privilege our cultural perspective over the teaching of the Bible. The second step is to remember that God shows us the best way to live since he is good. With that confidence in the goodness of God's word, the third step, then, is to test ideas and perspectives on the subject against what God explicitly says to us in Scripture. Some aspects of the Bible's teaching will resonate with our culture (for example, men and women are both in the image of God, have equal value and equal access to God and salvation, and so on). Others will challenge it (for example, the equality of men and women is strengthened, not diminished, by the differences between them, and these differences extend to what is appropriate and inappropriate in the exercise of ministry).

3. We hold this as a secondary but important issue

All truth matters, but not all doctrines are of the same weight and significance. It is important to get this clear.

First-order issues or doctrines: These are those necessary for salvation, and they form part of the historic orthodox faith—for example, the doctrine that the only way to be saved is by faith in Jesus Christ's death on the cross for your sin. Rejection of first-order doctrines are ultimately a rejection of true Christianity—those who reject them are not saved.

Second-order issues or doctrines: These are important issues that impact the life of the church both in the short term and in the long term—for example, the nature of the Lord's Supper or teaching on baptism. Christians who have come to different conclusions on these issues usually diverge into different churches, but they would still call each other a Christian brother or sister.

Third-order issues or doctrines: Christians may have different opinions on these, but they ought not to be held to be so fundamental as to make living alongside one another in the same local church too difficult. An example is the question of whether or not it is appropriate to drink alcohol.

Such definitions appear very neat, but in reality, the distinctions are often hard to draw.

So where does complementarianism fit? Clearly, you are not saved by what you believe about the relationship between men and women. In that sense it is not a first-order issue. Yet it is important. Given the question is directly addressed in the Bible, we cannot dismiss it as just a matter of personal choice. It certainly has big implications for the way we do church life. What is more, if in arguing for one side or another we end up dismissing parts of the Bible, or allowing them to be reinterpreted out of all recognition to the words actually written on the page, then we have a much more fundamental problem (see point 1)!

4. We respect people's conscience in application

Whenever we approach the topic of complementarianism, our consciences, and those of other people, are important considerations. No one has the right to bind another person's conscience more tightly than the word of God does. We need to respect each other's consciences, especially in details on which the Bible is silent or gives us freedom (1 Corinthians 10:27-29). Often among those who identify as complementarians, the differences of opinion are not so much about what the biblical passages are saying (although, of course, there is that) but rather about what complementarianism looks like in practice. We do not all have to come to the same conclusion in every area of practice! So, when we are in conversation with someone who differs from us on this issue—but who, nevertheless, delights in God's good word and wants it to shape the way they practise Christian ministry—we need to keep the conversation going and yet avoid walking all over each other's consciences. We need to learn how to live with difference in these cases.

Wherever we are on the spectrum of what the ministries of men and women look like in practice, we need to continually come back to God's word, so that our consciences can be aligned to and changed by what God is saying. As we do so, we will find that there is so much scope for what complementarianism can look like that approaches will be varied, even among churches that share the four convictions we have just outlined. It is in this spirit of humility that we continue.

REFLECTION QUESTIONS
For individuals
1. What are your immediate feelings and questions about complementarianism?
2. What has been your experience of church life in this area?
3. What aspects of your personal history shape your thinking and feeling?
4. Which of the concerns described resonate with you? Why?
5. Do you agree with the four principles as to how we approach this issue? Which might you struggle with?

For a group
1. What do members of our church instinctively think about complementarianism?
2. What stories would people tell about their experience and why?
3. Where do we fall short with regards to the four concerns raised?
4. What issues would come up if we discussed this as a leadership? As a church?
5. Where do we stand as a church on the four principles as to how we approach this issue?

2.

Men and Women Today

"**M**en and women are not the same and won't be the same, but that doesn't mean women shouldn't be treated fairly." So said the Canadian psychology professor and author Jordan Peterson in an interview with Cathy Newman on Channel 4 News in the UK, which quickly went viral and has since been watched over 7 million times online. Newman was questioning Peterson on men and women in society today. She pressed into issues like the masculinity crisis and the gender pay gap. She was on the offensive, claiming that Peterson had said some outrageous and untrue things. Peterson pushed back by saying it wasn't as simple as many people made out; men and women were different, he said, and that made a difference in life. It was fascinating viewing, and it starts to capture something of the turmoil around gender in the West today.

It's helpful for Christians to grapple with gender debates in our culture for at least three reasons. First, this is where we live and, like it or not, we will be affected by it. Churches absorb much of the thinking of the world, and so it's helpful to identify the key issues and ask to what extent we've bought into them. Second, we live out our faith in the world, and so knowing what people around us are currently thinking helps us to witness to them more thoughtfully. Third, the culture around us may put its finger on things, or ask questions, that we are blind to—and we may have something to learn as a result.

THE BATTLE OF THE SEXES

Two recently coined terms illustrate something of the current battle of the sexes. "Mansplaining" is when a man speaks in a patronising manner to a woman because he assumes she doesn't understand the subject under discussion. This term spotlights what has been a common tendency among men to think that they know more than women, especially about certain subjects, or that women wouldn't "get it" unless it was explained carefully.

Then there's the term "toxic masculinity", which has a mixed history but usually refers to a blend of masculine traits that form a toxic mix, such as competitiveness, dominance, and aggression. Again, it identifies something that can happen when a group of men interact with each other, and with women, in less than pleasant ways. But this isn't limited to laddish guys in the pub—it can be found in church offices too. Graham once joined a church staff team where his arrival changed the dynamic of the group, such that some of the women felt there was now a "competitiveness" within the team that there hadn't been previously. The men involved, however, were oblivious to this change. Being alert to such matters can only be helpful for anyone interested in mutual respect between the sexes, let alone basic Christian virtues such as kindness and gentleness.

However, despite what have seemed like advances in equality and fair treatment of women in society, there seems to be a never-ending succession of events that reveal how far there is to go. Scandals have emerged over unequal pay where men were clearly paid more than their female counterparts for the same role. More shocking has been the avalanche of allegations of sexual assault that have surfaced in the #MeToo movement. The ongoing abuse of power and position by men, to the detriment and abuse of women, is sickening.

As a result, the prevailing narrative in our culture is often that men need to realise their faults once again, own their sexism and "repent". In fact, it can sound as if you are guilty simply by being a man. At which point, we should be prompted to pause and ask some questions. While male sexism certainly still exists and we need to be aware of its current forms, it can't all be one-sided.

So, if we take the examples of "mansplaining" and "toxic masculinity", we might agree that they exist but question the asymmetry. Women are perfectly capable of being patronising to men, even if they may show it in different ways—perhaps by being dismissive rather than giving an overly detailed explanation. And is there not an equivalent mix of female traits which can also be toxic in some way—such as female cattiness rather than competitiveness? The Christian should quickly see that it is sin which is toxic, not gender. We may indeed sin in particular ways according to our gender and culture but, as Jesus says, it is our hearts which are the source of evil in the world (Mark 7:17-23). Rather than pitting men against women, we need to see how we have all turned against God, and then how that flows out between the two sexes.

Despite this "equality" in sin, we must still recognise that there has been an asymmetry historically, since men have been in a greater position of power and so have had opportunity for more overt forms of sin. But it is not as simple as "men are the problem".

Our culture's current conversations around gender highlight that even our supposedly equal, fair and tolerant Western society has further to travel. From a Christian point of view, we should not be surprised. Sexism, abuse and injustice are manifestations of sin—and while their particular guises will vary in type and severity, they will not be eradicated, because sin won't be eradicated until Jesus returns. We must still engage in the fight against them, but we know the battle won't end; it will only morph into new forms.

The question for the church, though, is this: do we recognise the fight? Do we think this is an issue for us within church or do we naively assume the church is a "sexist-free" zone, where such "gendered sin" doesn't exist? We need to look in the mirror, see our own faults, and make sure we've diagnosed the disease properly rather than just seeing the symptoms.

GENDER, JUSTICE AND IDENTITY

One reason why gender has become such a contentious issue today is because of the way in which it connects with other ideals that we hold as precious, particularly justice and the right to self-identity.

Justice has been a long-standing issue raised by feminism. It's helpful to draw a distinction here between "equity feminism" and "gender feminism". Equity feminism opposes discrimination based on sex so that there is fair treatment in all of life. Its history is in liberal and humanist thought. This was the focus of the early feminism of the 19th and 20th centuries, which sought to redress discrimination and campaigned for women's right to vote, to own property, to receive education, and to receive equal pay and benefits in employment. Later equity feminism pushed against confining the woman's role to the home and sought to widen women's access to stereotypically "male" professions. It often had a "whatever a man can do, a woman can do just as well" feel to it. Why shouldn't a woman be an accountant or a doctor?

Gender feminism is very different in that it seeks to eliminate differences between the sexes. It believes all such differences are socially constructed and must be done away with. It views interactions in terms of power and sees men as still dominating women. Liberation will be achieved not by pushing for equality but by the elimination of gender as a category. Its history is in Marxism and postmodern thought.

Evangelicals have sometimes been wary of calls for social justice and suspicious of the feminist movement. Some of that is entirely justified, but in this, at least, we should be clear: God is against unjust discrimination on the basis of sex. Our culture may take this to an extreme in some cases, and the cries of "Foul!" may be very loud, but the point made by equity feminism stands.

When it comes to gender feminism, though, the Bible disagrees, as we will show in the next chapter. But it is worth understanding why such issues are felt so deeply. It primarily comes down to people's understanding of identity. Contemporary Western culture emphasises that we are individuals and each have a unique identity, and that one of the most important things we must do is to embrace and express that identity. Nothing must be allowed to prevent that.

We see this most fully in the debates over transgender, and the right of someone who is biologically male to identify as a woman (or vice versa). This is what Carl Trueman calls the "triumph" of the modern self: we get to determine ourselves in any way we wish, including our gender. "Coming out" as trans or non-binary is celebrated by many as an act of personal authenticity.[2] Meanwhile, others are concerned to fight against what they see as the obliteration of sex differences, and especially to protect women against new forms of disadvantage and danger that may result. It is these deeply held feelings over identity that supercharge the debate over gender.

WHAT MAKES US MALE AND FEMALE?

The interview with Jordan Peterson to which we referred at the start of this chapter highlights another key question: to what extent are men and women the same, or different? Most people accept that there are biological differences in reproductive organs, height, body shape, and so on (although those are downplayed and even denied by some). But are there others?

The differences we're talking about here are often referred to as personality traits. There have been countless studies which have shown consistent differences between the sexes. These studies vary in their precise findings but show an overall repeatable picture, including across different cultures.[3] In general, men are found to tend towards greater competitiveness, dominance, risk-taking, initiation, and aggression, whereas women have greater empathy, intuition, and social skills. Other studies use different categories and show, for example, that men tend to be more goal orientated while women are personal-needs-orientated; or that men make closer peer bonds while women make closer family bonds. While most studies are on traits, some have looked at abilities, finding, for example, that overall men are better at three-dimensional conception, while women are better at verbal expression.

What these studies show is that there are clear differences between men and women on average, but with significant overlaps. Imagine plotting the height of every man and woman in the country on a graph (height on the horizontal X axis and number of men or women on the vertical Y axis). You'd get two overlapping curves each shaped like a "bell". Men on average would be undeniably taller, but the curves would overlap because some tall women are taller than shorter men. That's the sort of picture these studies paint when it comes to personality traits: there are true differences on average, but with significant overlap. Hence you can say, "On average men/women are…" but you can't say, "Every man/woman is…".

These differences in traits lead into differences in preferences. Take, for instance, the fact that there are far more male engineers and far more female nurses or more men in mathematics and more women in human resources. There has been a longstanding push in many countries to counter these trends, but they remain stubbornly resistant. Some differences may be because of, for instance, biases in education and recruitment, but it is increasingly accepted that they also stem from differences in personality traits and so in preferences. More women *want* to be nurses than men do.[4]

There are very mixed feelings about these sorts of findings in our culture today, though; in fact, to raise them is usually to invite severe pushback. As the psychologist Steven Pinker says, it's not hard to see why:

> *Why are people so afraid of the idea that the minds of men and women are not identical in every respect? ... The fear, of course, is that different implies unequal—that if the sexes differed in any way, then men would be have to be better, or more dominant, or have all the fun.*[5]

Given the precedent set by much of human history, we should sympathise with this instinct; men do not have a good track record on this score. They have too easily thought themselves better, been dominant, and made sure that they have had more fun. Yet even here we should note it is not all one way—the millions of servicemen killed and injured in the great conflicts of the 20th century were hardly having "fun". The key issue, though, is does "different" have to mean "unequal"? We say not. And while it is culturally and politically incorrect to say it, science continues to demonstrate that women and men tend towards different traits, abilities, and preferences.

We should also note that just because studies show certain differences, that doesn't mean that those differences are all necessarily good. From a Christian view, some traits are present because of sin. But even then, these still reveal differences—while all men and women are equally sinful, on average they sin in slightly different ways. Take the sinful tendency to jockey for position in a group at the expense of others. Men are more likely to use their achievements or physical prowess. Women tend to use verbal put-downs or snubs. It's the same sin filtered through gender. We can see this in a stark way in prison populations. In the UK the prison population is 95% male; in the US, it is 90%; in Australia, 92%.[6] That reflects something about men and their propensity to commit violence, theft and drug offences. That doesn't mean women are less sinful, but in sinning they simply do less that's illegal.

NATURE OR NURTURE?

So there do seem to be differences, on average, between the sexes. But that raises another question: where do they come from? Are gender differences hard-wired into us, or are we programmed by our upbringing? Is it nature or nurture?

The early feminist Simone de Beauvoir made the assertion that "one is not born, but rather becomes a woman".[7] The idea is that gender is socially constructed rather than innate.

Western culture today leans heavily towards this "social construction" view. Our "nature" is said to be plastic and flexible, and so any differences are because of the influences which are brought to bear on us as children and by the ongoing societal norms around us as adults. To counteract this there are increasing moves towards "neutral" parenting, which involves the strict avoidance of gender stereotyping—resulting in frustration if girls nevertheless end up liking pink and boys like fighting.

By contrast, a belief in innate differences assumes that there is something hard-wired into us as male or female, such that gender will emerge by itself. Some dissenting voices in Western culture still argue that this is the case and call out what they see as the madness of gender neutrality.[8]

Even if you think gender differences are innate, you may also think socialisation has a shaping effect. It can be both/and rather than either/or. As one Christian author puts it:

> *Social construction of gender is real, but it operates with the natural reality of difference between the sexes, rather than creating difference* ex nihilo *[out of nothing]. The exact shape of the gendered differences between men and women varies considerably from culture to culture, yet the presence of a gender distinction between men and women is universal.*[9]

Again, any suggestion that there are innate differences between men and women often raises hackles instantly. In Western culture we tend to be suspicious of such thoughts because they so often go hand in hand with stereotyping, superiority and inequality. But that need not be the case. As Pinker says:

> *Of course, just because many sex differences are rooted in biology does not mean that one sex is superior, that the differences will emerge for all people in all circumstances, that discrimination against a person based on sex is justified, or that people should be coerced into doing things typical of their sex. But neither are the differences without consequences.*[10]

We live in a stubbornly gendered world, and that shapes the experience of being a man or a woman in it. If these differences are there because of how God has made us, then "going with the grain" of his design will actually be good for us—and help us to truly be ourselves.

THE DEBATES IN THE CHURCH

Those are some of the debates being had in our culture on the nature of gender. Now we're ready to narrow in on some of the parallel debates among complementarian churches.

God's commands and gender

The discussion over complementarianism has usually focused on Bible passages that give different roles for men and women within church and family. As important as it is to understand *what* God commands in these areas, it's also important to ask *why*? Why does God prohibit women from being elders or call men to take the lead in the home? Is it because men are innately more suited to it?

Some authors occasionally venture into this territory. For example, one writer, having described the Bible's requirement for male leadership in church, questioned why God had prohibited this role to women. He pondered as to whether women were more gullible than men. Upon hearing this explanation, Graham's wife responded, "So why can they teach children and other women? Is it ok for the gullible to teach the more gullible?!" The author I'm thinking of subsequently retracted his comment, saying they were well meant but far too speculative (which is one reason why he's not named here). That goes to illustrate the dangerous ground we're on in making global comments about gender.

Broad and narrow views of gender

This leads to a question about the *scope* of the Bible's teaching on gender. Some authors and teachers have said that God only specifies gender roles for certain areas of life, namely marriage and church leadership, and that the Bible's teaching does not extend to other areas, such as the secular workplace. So complementarianism shouldn't try to be all encompassing; it should stick to those specific roles. This can be thought of as a "narrow" view of gender.

Meanwhile others have said that we are male and female across all of life, 24/7, and so gender differences permeate everything. If we limit gender differences to specific roles, then we're in danger of saying, "I am now a man/woman" only when those roles are in play. This "broad" view of gender sees God's specific commands in Scripture about marriage and church leadership as the tip of a gender iceberg; they are the most obvious manifestation of it, but there's lots more going on under the surface.

This debate is easily seen in a brief online exchange. The pastor and author John Piper answered the question, "Should women be police officers?" on his *Ask Pastor John* podcast.[11] He outlined his view of men's responsibility to lead and women's affirmation of that leadership. While he thought this would look very different depending on the type of relationship in question, he nonetheless saw it applying to *all* male-female relationships, not just those in marriage and church leadership. With regard to the actual question about police officers, Piper was cautious not to be definitive, but his answer seemed to lean towards "no", because the role of a police officer could involve exercising directive, personal leadership over a man. Hence Piper was seeing gender roles in the "broad" sense above.

Author Aimee Byrd wrote an article in response to Piper's answer, arguing that it wasn't biblical. Her point was that God has specified complementary roles for marriage and church leadership, and not any other context. So, she said, we mustn't try to overextend those principles into the rest of life.[12] Theologian Carl Trueman backed Byrd up, saying of complementarian teaching, "I felt it lost its way when it became an all-embracing view of the world and not simply a matter for church and household."[13] This is the "narrow" view of gender and its roles.

In this "specific roles only" camp, there is a tendency to downplay the shaping of "gender" at large, and less concern to detail what masculinity and femininity might comprise. The focus is on getting the specific roles right. They are also less likely to connect these roles with any innate differences.

By contrast, in the broad "all of life" camp, the tendency is to play up gender and its influence everywhere. This group are more likely to try to define male and female characteristics, and may start to say that men are "like this" while women are "like that". So, for instance, you expect male engineers and female nurses, and you don't try to change that because you'd be fighting nature. Gender is innate and flows out everywhere.

The strength of the "specific role" narrow group is that they are most clearly working directly from Scripture: God gives some specific commands, so they say we should simply stick to those and not extrapolate from them to anywhere else. The weakness is that those commands seem to be isolated islands that have little to do with being men or women generally.

The strength of the "all of life" broad group is that they see the specific commands as the tip of the iceberg: they represent the most obvious part of a substructure of how God has designed gender. So, the commands God gives aren't arbitrary, but are more of a piece with creation at large. The weakness of this group is that they seem to make some generalised statements about gender that the Bible doesn't.

Unbalanced complementarianism?

This discussion within the complementarian camp has involved other concerns as well. The first concern is that traditional complementarianism has been overly focused on the authority of men and submission of women, to the harm and detriment of women.[14] The "broad" view above could end up saying that all women should submit to all men; or even that leadership and submission are the very substance of gender differences. That is very different to saying that God intends for there to be leadership and submission within particular relationships.

A second concern is that the patterns of interaction between men and women in churches today are simply traditional rather than biblical. Sometimes complementarians are only reflecting, and defending, cultural norms from a by-gone era, and the result is overly restrictive and limiting of women.

Rachel Green Miller reflects both of those concerns:

> *As theologically conservative Christians, we must acknowledge where extrabiblical and unbiblical ideas about women and men have permeated, weakened, and confused our teachings. We need to move beyond a focus on authority and submission in order to incorporate equally important biblical themes into our discussions, such as unity, interdependence, and service. As we do, we will strengthen our vital relationship as co-labourers in Christ.*[15]

SUMMARY

So that's where we in the West find ourselves. Our culture is deeply conflicted about gender. It is seen as almost irrelevant to who we are, what we can do and what we're like, and yet at the same time gender is a deeply held part of our identity. Our culture longs for justice and equality between the sexes but struggles to make that happen or even know what that looks like.

And we're conflicted within the church, too. Why does God command what he does? Is God's concern with gender differences limited to the roles of church and family, or should we take a broader view? Is the concern with authority and submission unhealthy and unbiblical?

Those are some of the questions we'll consider as we turn to what the Bible says about gender.

REFLECTION QUESTIONS
For individuals
1. What differences do you instinctively feel exist between men and women?
2. What have you experienced within the wider culture of the gender debates? How have they made you feel?
3. Do you think differences between the sexes are from nature or nurture?
4. What did you make of the difference between "narrow" and "broad" complementarianism?
5. Do you know what position you take?

For a group
1. What differences do we think there are between men and women?
2. How are such differences seen in our church?
3. Does our church hold to a "narrow" or "broad" complementarianism, or is it not clear?
4. Are we more in danger of defending traditional views above biblical teaching or of bowing to our culture?
5. What areas of confusion do we feel as a church?

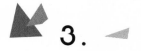

3.

How Are We Made?

"Women get too emotional."

So said someone following a church leaders' meeting. The church in question was led by a group of male elders overseeing spiritual life and male deacons overseeing practical issues, although there were some women on staff. At that time, both the eldership and diaconate were restricted to men, but there was an ongoing discussion about whether women should be permitted to serve as deacons. In this particular leaders' meeting, there was a debate about some other issue that got rather tense, and a female staff member who was present became upset and cried. So it was that after the meeting one of the deacons said, "This is why we don't want women serving as deacons—they get too emotional."

How would you respond?

Although the passages we're about to look at are probably very familiar, they are foundational to how we think about men and women. How we respond to this and multiple other situations in church life will ultimately come back to this question: how are we made?

CREATION: SIMILAR AND DIFFERENT

The first key passage for us comes in Genesis 1:

> *26 Then God said, "Let us make mankind in our image, in our likeness, so that they may rule over the fish in the sea*

and the birds in the sky, over the livestock and all the wild animals, and over all the creatures that move along the ground."

27 So God created mankind in his own image, in the image of God he created them; male and female he created them.

28 God blessed them and said to them, "Be fruitful and increase in number; fill the earth and subdue it. Rule over the fish in the sea and the birds in the sky and over every living creature that moves on the ground."

(Genesis 1:26-28)

Human beings are made in God's image, and this gives us a distinct and privileged role in creation; people bear God's image "so that they may rule" (v 26), and that leads to the commands to "fill the earth and subdue it" and "rule over" it (v 28). So, imaging God is about the role we play in ruling the world on his behalf.

Equality

For our purposes, one important thing to see is that both men and women are made in God's image. The reference to "mankind" (or "man" in some versions) in verses 26 and 27 is to all of humanity. (The word "man" is used generically for the human race as a whole.) In verse 27 there is then reference to the two sub-groups of "mankind"—that is, "male and female" (using different words). So, both male and female are part of "mankind", and both are made in God's image. This means there is an equality in dignity and value between men and women; we are equally made in God's image to rule his world together. But it goes further: there is also profound unity between men and women—we together, as one humanity, form the image of God to rule his world.

So while men and women are obviously different in lots of ways (and we'll get to those), the first thing we should note is a unity and similarity. The writer Dorothy Sayers put it well:

> *The first thing that strikes the careless observer is that women are unlike men. They are the "opposite sex" ... But the fundamental thing is that women are more like men than anything else in the world. They are human beings.*[16]

That similarity and equality between men and women might seem obvious to us, but it is of profound importance. It counters any thinking that women are "lesser"—a line of thought which does, unfortunately, have a long history to it, even within the church. Some Christian writers from previous centuries said that men bore the image of God fully and that women either didn't bear it themselves or did so in a partial way.

There are more subtle forms of thinking of women as "lesser" as well; some have thought of men as "normal" and women as a "variation on male". Such variation is then seen as "worse". But Genesis 1 rules out that sort of thinking: there is "mankind", which is then equally differentiated into "male" and "female". This is the creation that God commends as "very good" (Genesis 1:31).

Distinction

Men and women, while similar, are not identical. Humanity can be divided by ethnicity, age, culture, ability or many other factors. But as significant as these may be, the only difference God gives us at this stage in Genesis is gender.

Whatever some quarters of society might say today about there being a spectrum of gender, the Bible is clear that it is binary: you are a woman or a man, and they are distinct. Yet, again, the Bible gives a picture of togetherness with difference; it's a wonderful blend of similarity and distinction, which we see repeated and nuanced in chapter 2:

18 The LORD God said, "It is not good for the man to be alone. I will make a helper suitable for him."

19 Now the LORD God had formed out of the ground all the wild animals and all the birds in the sky. He brought them to the man to see what he would name them; and whatever the man called each living creature, that was its name. 20 So the man gave names to all the livestock, the birds in the sky and all the wild animals.

But for Adam no suitable helper was found. 21 So the LORD God caused the man to fall into a deep sleep; and while he was sleeping, he took one of the man's ribs and then closed up the place with flesh. 22 Then the LORD God made a woman from the rib he had taken out of the man, and he brought her to the man.

23 The man said,
"This is now bone of my bones
and flesh of my flesh;
she shall be called 'woman',
for she was taken out of man."

24 That is why a man leaves his father and mother and is united to his wife, and they become one flesh.

25 Adam and his wife were both naked, and they felt no shame. (Genesis 2:18-25)

The shock in verse 18 is that something was not good in creation—the man was alone. It's not that God had come across an inadvertent problem in his creation that he now needed to fix. Rather, this is teaching us the absolute necessity of women. And it's not simply that Adam would have felt lonely; it's that the man, by himself, could not fulfil God's creation purposes.

So the search began for a "suitable" helper. This too underlines the similarity between men and women again. The point of the parade of animals is not that God really thought Adam would find such a companion among the animals ("How about the giraffe?"); rather, the fruitless search among the animals emphasises that none of them were suitable because they were too different from Adam.

Not so the woman. She is created from part of Adam's own body; she is, he declares, "bone of my bones and flesh of my flesh". In other words, *She is suitable for me precisely because she is from me and so is like me.* The companionship between the sexes hinges on, and requires, their similarity and equality. If we think of women, or men, as lesser beings in any way, then we immediately undermine real relationships between the sexes. Men and women are pictured here as being of the same "flesh", one made from the other, and recognised as such. And so again there is a profound unity between us.

But we also see difference between men and women. The woman is not another man. The companionship between the sexes also turns on, and requires, their difference. The key phrase here is that the man needs someone "suitable for him" (v 18). A more literal rendering of this phrase is "like-opposite to him". It implies a correspondence where something is fitting but also different. It is "like" but is also "opposite". It's like jigsaw puzzle pieces that fit together, precisely because they are similar but different, and their differences correspond with each other.

This similarity and difference are seen in Adam's naming of the woman: he is *ish* (man), and she is *ishshah* (woman)—words that are similar yet different. And it's also seen in their physical biology—men and women "fit together" physically in sex. That is a key part of their suitability for each other because God's plan and command is for them to "be fruitful and increase in number" (1:28). We're not told here in Genesis what other differences there might be between men and women beyond biology. We're just given this simple principle:

we are made of the same stuff and so we are similar, but we are also made different and so we are complementary.

Helper?

So what about the term "helper" (v 18, 20)? In English that sounds subservient or demeaning, and Genesis 2 has been taken that way by some. So is it? No.

First, we need to remember what Genesis 1 said about equality in God's image and in God's task, and not overturn that here; this may add to that picture, but it will not contradict it. Second, we need to know that the word "helper" need not have any sense of inferiority to it. It's a word that's used of God as the "helper" of his people (for example, in Psalm 33:20), and God certainly isn't inferior to them. As the writer Claire Smith says, "The point is that those needing help cannot do it on their own. So it is for the man."[17]

But third, the idea of a "helper" does seem to fit with distinguishing roles. The man is created first and then the woman, so she joins him in the task already given, and he is the one who names her. The fact that Adam was created first is taken by Paul in the New Testament as a basis for male leadership or headship in some of the passages we'll consider later (1 Corinthians 11:2-16; 1 Timothy 2:11-15). So while the ordering of creation doesn't mean women are inferior in any way, it does point us to a difference in relationships and roles.

Two dangers to avoid

So in Genesis 1 – 2 we see a wonderful blend of similarity and difference. There are two immediate dangers to avoid. The first is the blurring of gender, where male and female are seen as the same, as if we are interchangeable. This denies the differences God has created. The second is the opposing of gender, where male and female are seen as wholly different. This sees them as so "other" that they cannot be companions or partners in any meaningful way. They are forever trapped in the "battle of the sexes", or at least have to separate and live in isolation. This overplays the differences and denies the similarity.

A lot of writing on gender leans in one of those two directions, but we must hold together similarity and difference as the basis of our relationship and unity.

DIFFERENT READINGS

It is at this stage that some of the differences between various complementarian positions start to emerge. All would agree that God makes men and women both similar and different, but some go on to unpack gender differences much more fully from these passages. For example, the writer and theologian Alastair Roberts makes these points:[18]

- Man is created first.
- Man can represent all of humanity (whereas woman does not).
- The image of God is especially focused on the man.
- The man is given the task of working the garden; the woman's "help" is for the sake of fruitfulness.
- The man is created outside the garden and has a special relationship with that "outside world"; the woman is made inside the garden and has a special relationship with that "inside world".
- The man's naming of animals and the woman is a sign of his ruling over the world.
- The man leaves his parents and joins with his wife because the bonds of human relationship are primarily formed by women.
- The fall affects the primary areas of responsibility: work for the man and child-bearing for the woman.

- The man relates to the first three of days of creation (in separating, ruling and naming); the woman relates to the second three (in filling and creating life).

The result is, according to Roberts, that men have an outward-facing responsibility, bring order, and are task-orientated; whereas women are more relational and nurturing and focused on the home.

Other authors also see the commission of 1:28 as giving greater specificity to men and women's roles.[19] While the command to rule is given to both sexes they each have a different "centre of gravity" in how to fulfil it. These sorts of readings usually go hand-in-hand with the "broad" view of gender we described in the last chapter.

The question is whether these sorts of details are in the text of Genesis 1 – 3 or whether they are an "over-reading". In our view, for example, it's not clear from these passages that women are more focused on the "inside world" or form the bonds of human relationship. We would agree that men are presented as overall leaders, and that that principle may filter down to give shape to some of the other distinctions, but we don't see such distinctions clearly there by themselves.

We've included this section, though, so that you can see where some complementarians are coming from and why they say what they do. Some of the differences in emphasis between complementarians flow from these differences in interpretation. We need to recognise this and humbly discuss the issues involved.

WHAT THIS MEANS FOR CHURCH LIFE
We've seen that men and women are made similar but different. That brings a number of implications to work through in church life.

Embodying equality

Men and women are equal. There are differences in roles, and there may be differences in personality traits, but these are undergirded by equality of value and significance before God. We must therefore long for our churches to be places that embody such equality. We say "embody" here because it is not enough to say we're equal or even to recognise that we're equal; it must be lived out in our life together, embodied in reality.

Sarah Sumner writes:

> *Christians don't have to be feminists in order to believe in social justice. Feminism is not something that must be added to Christianity in order for the church to honor women. The gospel itself is pro-women ... Anyone who thinks that treating women fairly is a feminist thing to do, not a Christian thing to do, doesn't understand Christianity.*[20]

We must recognise our own history here and the tendency there has been to think of women as inferior. We've mentioned that some people have taught that women do not bear God's image as fully as men. Others have cast them as dangerous temptresses, because sin came into the world through them; or have viewed women as incomplete until married but seen single men as fine as they are. It's these trains of thought that lead Sumner to point out that the call to recognise the equal worth of women is actually a novel voice in church history.[21]

Many of us must go further in speaking out against sexism or misogyny—otherwise the underlying message is that it's ok or not that bad. But it's not merely a case of talking about equality, but living it out together. Some sexism that denigrates women is overt and obvious, but much of it is more subtle. It is about assumptions we make and tendencies we have, which we may not be very aware of. The term used today is "unconscious bias": a blind spot where you don't see how you are prejudiced in some way.

One online article described the experience of Sara, a highly qualified woman who worked in a research laboratory and had done so with success for many years. And yet...

> *There were a thousand little ways Sara was reminded of her second-class status at work. She was regularly mistaken for a secretary by employees from other labs, and by people calling the office phone. She was chronically interrupted by every man she worked with from her boss down to the summer interns. Every conversation was an opportunity for men to talk over her, assume she didn't know what she was talking about, question her expertise, and then explain her own job to her. It didn't matter that she had years of proven success in that position with more experience than most of the men around her. They assumed on reflex that she didn't know anything.*[22]

Imagine being treated like that (especially if you are a man reading this). Think about being patronised and about people assuming unfair things about you, purely because of your sex. The article went on to speak about how women in the workplace wanted men of moral integrity who were prepared to lose some social capital in front of their peers by the way in which they honoured women. What a great thing to call for—what a Christian thing to call for.

I (Graham) expect though that many or even all of the men Sara interacted with were blind to what they were doing—it was an unconscious bias. What worries me is whether there are ways in which I may exhibit such bias in the way that I treat all kinds of people, including women. For example, I recently organised a meeting of small-group leaders at our church. I circulated a date, but a couple of the female leaders weren't able to make the meeting time. As it was only a couple, I decided to go ahead with the meeting anyway. Then someone helpfully asked if I would have done the same if a few of the male leaders hadn't been able to be there. I'm honestly not sure what the answer would have been—but it was a penetrating and challenging question.

Each year at the theological college where I (Jane) work, we go on a week-long mission. The students are divided into small groups which are each led by a male and female co-chaplain. These mission teams go to various churches, across different denominations, within Australia and overseas. Yet on several of the missions where I have co-led, the pastor of the host church has spoken about the mission team purely as if it were led by the male co-chaplain. So, for instance, when one pastor thanked the team for coming, he thanked my co-chaplain and said nothing to me. It is a weird experience feeling as if someone does not recognise that you exist, even though you are right in front of them. I wanted to ask him, "What message does that send to our students, both male and female, about how to view your sisters and female co-workers in Christ?"

In an article entitled "Three Female Ghosts That Haunt the Church", Jen Wilkin describes three "ghosts" which connect with particular forms of common bias. They are women as "usurpers", who are reaching for power; women as "temptresses", who are dangerous to men; and women as "children", who need to be handled gently and are usually patronised as a result. These forms of unconscious bias can shape men's reaction to women, and women's view of themselves.[23]

We need to recognise that these kinds of bias exist and that they undercut our equality. We should also recognise that it can be very hard for women to point them out because they may feel that to do so would be seen to be criticising men or promoting themselves, or would put them at risk of being labelled with a stereotype such as the "difficult" woman.

The theme of unconscious bias can be taken too far: people, especially men, can be made to feel that they must be doing something wrong, but they're too thick to see it, and so it must be pointed out to them. It can breed suspicion, so that anyone who is male is considered guilty from the off—which is, of course, its own form of bias.

In the church, though, we should surely have the humility to know we may be biased and not see it, and the generosity to think well of people rather than assuming the worst.

Honouring difference

Second, we need to honour the differences that there are between men and women. We've said one historical move is to assume that men are normal and then to judge women according to the extent to which they measure up. That is not respecting difference. Respecting difference means that we expect women to bring something different, rather than only replicate men, so we won't penalise women when they do things differently. Again, we must remember there is overlap, too—so women are not entirely and only different. But there is complementarity. And when we lean into that, both men and women are affirmed and dignified.

This honouring of difference also means we won't resort to unhelpful caricatures. The caricatures are there because of the differences—men and women do have certain tendencies. But if we respect differences, we don't turn them into caricatures to be used against each other. That is what is happening if women complain about how "clueless" men are, or men about how "emotional" women are.

Here's the danger for many men: to think of any differences women display as a variant away from "normal" and therefore worse. What we should want to think is "God has made us different, and there is something good and right and enriching about those differences, so I am glad of them, honour them and welcome them".

Honouring difference will also show itself in ministry. The danger here is that we will only honour women for how much they do ministry like men do; and, potentially, think negatively of them for the ways in which their ministry differs. Sarah Sumner writes honestly about realising how she had bought into this way of thinking:

> *Although I am a woman, I have tacitly thought of myself as a special type of woman, the kind that can keep up with men.*[24]

She says she realised she was just as guilty of the instinctive pride and prejudice she saw in many men. There will, of course, be lots of similarities between women and men in ministry, but there will be differences, and we want to embrace and honour them. It's not that male is right and female has to fit in. Sam Andreades writes of two tests for our churches:

> *Here are two tests to measure women's status in your setting: (1) If a woman feels the need to self-censor any female issues or feminine attitudes in order to be taken seriously, your practice is skewed and unbiblical in how it distinguishes gender. (2) If women are marginalized by the structures of operation, we have a great deal to answer for to God, since we are disobeying the very first chapter of the Bible.*[25]

WHAT WOULD YOU SAY?

So let's go back to the deacon who said, "This is why we don't want women serving as deacons—they get too emotional". Whether or not you believe that it is biblically appropriate for women to serve as deacons, this comment nonetheless reveals some unhelpful attitudes. So what could you lovingly say in response? Maybe...

- that expressing emotion was appropriate given the topic of the conversation—and so maybe the men present should be challenged to show some emotion rather than most of them remaining unmoved.

- that he was making a sweeping generalisation in thinking all women would act in a similar way.
- that even if many women would be more emotionally attuned and expressive, that might actually be a good thing to complement a male perspective.
- that the men might have their own tendencies in how they responded, such as being competitive or argumentative, of which they were unaware.
- that he was thinking of men as "normal" and women as "lesser" because of this difference.

We've seen how God makes us: equal but distinct. We've seen some indication of differences between the sexes. And we've started to grapple with the resulting equality and difference in church life. I hope you see already that the Bible gives a true picture of who we are, and that the foundation is laid for a wonderfully rich and united life together. That's what we need to explore further.

REFLECTION QUESTIONS

For individuals

1. What should we learn from the accounts of creation about men and women?
2. Do you tend to think more in terms of similarity or distinction between men and women?
3. In what ways might you think of men as "normal" and women as "lesser"?
4. What is so true and attractive about the biblical picture we've explored in this chapter?

For a group

1. What tendencies does our church have in thinking about men and women?
   a. Does it emphasise both similarity and distinction?
   b. Does it make men "normal" and women "lesser"?
2. What is your experience, as a man or a woman, in terms of the expectations placed on you or the treatment you've received?
3. What truths in this chapter might we want to embody more fully as a church or ministry team? Discuss some examples of what that embodiment might look like.
4. What would be good about being part of a church that gets this right?

4.
God's Call to Men and Women

The BBC radio programme *Woman's Hour* recently had a discussion on "Being a man today". It was fascinating. Some guests drew attention to poor forms of masculinity, such as over-competitiveness and arrogance. Another asserted that being a man could mean "anything" depending on who you are. And yet, there was also a persistent feeling that there is something specific to being a man—and while everyone agreed, no one quite said what it was. I expect a parallel discussion on being a woman today would have a similar feel. We know men and women are different, but we're not sure how.

Now imagine a Christian radio show having a similar panel discussion where the subject is "Being a *Christian* man today" or "Being a *Christian* woman today". What sort of answers might be given? What sort of answer would *you* give?

The previous chapter laid out the two broad principles of embodying equality and honouring difference. But that still leaves us with lots of questions: What does it mean to be male and female, beyond the obvious physical differences? Aside from the "roles" of pastor, or husband or wife, does gender come into our Christian lives at all? Crucially, does discipleship look any different for a man and a woman? This is a challenging area to write on, and the answers are hard to pin down. One writer likened the difference between men and women to different perfumes: you know the difference when you smell them, but it's very difficult to describe. This chapter is our attempt to describe those scents nevertheless!

THE TWO COMMON DANGERS

There are dangers on both sides of the road when it comes to this area. First is the danger of *overemphasising* the differences between men and women. Imagine again that hypothetical radio panel—some people would happily paint specific, and quite different, pictures of discipleship for men and women. One person might speak of women as captivating princesses and men as gallant warriors who will sweep them off their feet. It's like a Christian version of an old Disney film that reflects certain stereotypes. Another panellist might talk of the need for Christian men to be "real men" who do "manly" things—so that a man listening might feel ashamed if he couldn't grow a decent beard or didn't like extreme sports. Corresponding to that might be the ideal Christian woman, who is supposed to love nothing more than being a "homemaker"—to the embarrassment of any woman who can't bake a decent cupcake.

These are caricatures of male and female that buy into particular cultural trends and preferences. They emphasise the differences between men and women, with the expectation that their lives look very different. You see this in the "Men are from Mars, Women are from Venus" type comments; we're set almost against each other. Whereas the truth is that we're both from Planet Earth and so have an awful lot in common. Along with the overemphasis on difference comes the tendency to specify particular ways in which we are *meant* to be different. This often leads to what's been called "performative identities", where we're given an identity to live up to and so feel the need to perform appropriately.

Definitions of gender like these usually reveal more about the preferences of those speaking than any biblical insight. As we'll see below, in the Bible men and women are never told to take on a particular personality type or set of interests based on their sex. Sam Andreades gives reassurance to those who feel they don't fit the stereotypes: "a woman who excels in mixed martial arts is not less of a woman".[26] So, he says, "let us rather applaud the wisdom of the Bible's teaching, not defining gender in terms of essential characteristics".

The opposite danger is that of *underemphasising* the differences between men and women. You could imagine a speaker on the panel responding to the caricatures above by saying that they are nonsense, and that there's nothing specific about being a man or a woman, so don't worry about it. They might say that God calls us all to be like Christ, and there's nothing more to it.

The desire to play down differences between men and women is understandable, particularly for those who've felt restricted by caricatures. One writer who felt the pressure of the performative identities reacted like this:

I am a human—in a male body. Nonetheless, it is a male body; it is what it is. My primary challenge is to define my human experience in such a way that I can be comfortable with my innate interests and characteristics, regardless of my anatomy.[27]

The writer, understandably, does not want his "maleness" to dictate his interests and personality. He goes on to conclude, "I have allowed my humanness to transcend my gender". But notice how this now starts to make our gender seem accidental and almost irrelevant to our personhood. As we've seen, the Genesis narrative places great emphasis on the fact that we are all human *and* that we are each male or female. So it would be better to say that our humanness is expressed *in* and *through* our gender. But what does that look like?

CALLED TO GODLINESS, NOT GENDER

As hinted at above, God doesn't give any gender-specific commands in the Bible to do with personality type, interests, or traits. Women are not told be gentle and nurturing or to like sewing, and men are not told to be directive and goal orientated or to like sport. While men and women do, on average, have certain personality traits, these are never commanded, and so we must be very careful not to say that they are what God *calls* men and women to be.

There *are* some gender-specific commands in the Bible, but they are all given with respect to certain relationships. For example, women are instructed not to have authority as church leaders over men, and husbands are told to love their wives (1 Timothy 2:12; Colossians 3:19). But these commands are for certain *dynamics in a relationship,* not for *certain personality types or interests.* It is really important to distinguish between these otherwise we will place unfair and unnecessary expectations on each other.

Graham knows one lady who has felt this very keenly. She is an extrovert who is full of energy and speaks her mind. However, she has been made to feel that she should not be like that and should become "quieter". While she should, of course, submit to her husband and her church leaders—and while a tendency to speak quickly and loudly means she might need to reflect on her reactions—such submission doesn't equate to a "quiet" personality. In fact, you could be naturally very quiet but very rebellious in your heart.

The overwhelming majority of commands in Scripture are directed to men and women equally. We are *all* told to be holy, loving, kind, gentle and humble. Men are told to be compassionate, just as much as woman are (Colossians 3:12); and women are told to be strong just as much as men are (1 Corinthians 16:13). We're all called to imitate Christ. As Michael Bird has observed, neither Jesus nor Paul "issue caveats that the imitation of Christ comes in pink and blue".[28]

So Scripture's main priority for the believer is not manliness or womanliness but godliness. Or we might say, God's concern is not with being a man or a woman but being Christ-like. This itself will immediately bring its own challenges to us as men and women. As we've already noted, the pernicious effects of sin mean that our "natural" setting isn't always the right one. Some of what might come more naturally to us as men or as women will need to be countered:

> *If it is more natural for a man to be aggressive and a woman to be passive, then a genuine encounter with Christ should challenge a man to become gentle (Gal. 5:23) and a woman to become bold (2 Tim. 1:7).*[29]

Nonetheless, the key point is that God calls all of us to godliness.

CALLED TO GODLINESS EXPRESSED THROUGH GENDER

This distinction between godliness and gender has sometimes been used on the side of those underemphasising gender: "God is only interested in godliness," we're told, "so don't worry about gender". Not so fast.

First, our godliness will be lived out in a gendered way. We've seen that there are, on average, differences between the sexes, and those will show themselves in our discipleship. The way in which we are kind, or express encouragement, or love our neighbour, and so on, will be shown *through* our gender—and that will, on average, look somewhat different between men and women. And that is a good, right and enriching thing to be embraced.

The reality is that we are never *not* a man or a woman— which means that we only ever express our godliness through our gender—it is part of who we are. So, for example, while we are all called to show compassion to one another, that compassion will be expressed with different words, actions, tone and expression. And so too will there be a different colouring to our encouragement, teaching, rebuking, and so on, because of our gender. That's not to say that the differences will always be obvious, or that there is simply a female or a male way of doing each of those things—there is great variety! But nonetheless, our gender will be part of what shapes the way we do them. And the differences that exist between men and women are for the good of humanity—differences that allow men and women to unite together in marriage, and to complement and aid each other in church community. They are therefore not to be viewed negatively or minimised. As Roberts says, "It's not about difference *from* each other, but difference *for* each other".[30]

Second, our godliness is expressed differently according to our roles in life. Jonathan Leeman says that when people say that we're called to be godly rather than gendered they are in danger of a "category error".[31] That is, by pitting the two against each other, it "confuses our ultimate goal of modelling Christ with the different ways God assigns us to do this". For example, children should be "godly", but they are also told to obey their parents (Ephesians 6:1); those two commands shouldn't be set against each other. In fact, obeying their parents is one way in which they will be godly. Similarly, in Titus 2 married women are to be taught to "love their husbands and children" (Titus 2:4). So being godly or Christ-like will take on a different shape depending on our life circumstances and the relationships we're in.

Leeman goes on to say:

Yet what if Christlikeness doesn't look like just one thing? What if there was a male kind and a female kind? A kind for the writer and the singer, the architect and the builder? The nine and 90-year-old? The Nigerian tribal chief and

the New York subway driver? The mother and the father?
The sister and the brother? The husband and the wife?
Might Christ's beauty refract just a little differently from
each of these angles? Offering a more resplendent display of
his glory, like a stained-glass cathedral window instead of
the monochromatic glum of a beer bottle? [32]

So, when we say the main concern of Scripture is not manliness or womanliness but godliness, we do not mean to use that to duck all the specific contexts in which we are called to be godly. And that will involve working out men's and women's roles within the family and the church.

Nevertheless, as we consider what God calls us to as men and women, we need to get our chronology right; we begin with the call to godliness given equally to all. Then we move to the second question: "What does being godly mean for me as a man or a woman, a husband, wife, mother, son, sister and so on?" And we need to get our perspective right: the aim is Christlikeness. That has implications for my roles in life, but the goal I am striving towards is to be like Jesus, rather than trying to measure up to a certain picture of a man or a woman.

The result is that there will be lots of similarities between us as well as differences. The potential danger of Leeman's illustration of the stained glass window is that we each make a distinct contribution of colour. That's true in as much as I am a distinct individual, but misleading in that I am trying to be Christ-like in very similar ways to every other believer. Perhaps we're more like an orchestra playing the same tune but on different instruments, each of which bring their own contribution. And even then, there are other people playing the same instrument as we are.

So instead of advocating those "performative identities" we mentioned earlier, let's encourage an organic living out of who we are and how God made us. That will look somewhat different for different people, including different men and women. It will also look different in different cultures. There is real freedom here—not a free-for-all, because we all look to obey God, but freedom from caricatures and from any one specific cultural embodiment. So if you, as a woman or a man, are looking to obey God in all your relationships, roles and responsibilities in life—if you are looking to be godly and follow the Lord Jesus—then be reassured that you are living the life God calls you to.

This is, then, where churches need to be very careful: in not painting extra-biblical pictures of manhood and womanhood, either by design or by default. This is what can sometimes happen when the events at church invariably involve crafts and baking for the women, and big breakfasts and long walks for the men; or when illustrations in talks or services use caricatures of roles. This can be difficult to navigate because there's nothing wrong with a craft evening for a group of women if that's what works! But we need to be wary of making assumptions and giving a picture that says, "This is what God calls you to".

CALLED TO DISCIPLESHIP

God calls men and women to be disciples of the Lord Jesus. The invitation to get to know him, love him, serve him, and follow him is given to both sexes. We must ensure that we see that very clearly and allow it to permeate our thinking and our churches.

First, we should note that this equality in discipleship is unusual. In 1st-century Israel, women were not equal in this way. Yet when Mary sat at Jesus' feet listening to him, she was commended by him (Luke 10:38-42). Jesus was very happy to have women as part of his wider grouping and to be dependent on them for provision (see Luke 8:1-3). On one occasion, he was told that his family were outside looking for him, and we read this:

> Then [Jesus] looked at those seated in a circle round him and said, "Here are my mother and my brothers! Whoever does God's will is my brother and sister and mother."
>
> (Mark 3:34-35)

When one woman showed her devotion to Jesus by anointing him with expensive perfume, Jesus said she had done "a beautiful thing to me". He went on: "Truly I tell you, wherever the gospel is preached throughout the world, what she has done will also be told, in memory of her" (Mark 14:3-9).

These examples show a welcome of and involvement with women that broke with tradition. Dorothy Sayers, a writer in the first half of the 20th century, looked at Jesus' attitude to women and reflected:

> Perhaps it is no wonder that the women were first at the Cradle and last at the Cross. They had never known a man like this Man—there never has been such another. A prophet and teacher who never nagged at them, never flattered or coaxed or patronised; who never made arch jokes about them, never treated them either as "The women, God help us!" or "The ladies, God bless them!"; who rebuked without querulousness and praised without condescension; who took their questions and arguments seriously; who never mapped out their sphere for them, never urged them to be feminine or jeered at them for being female; who had no axe to grind and no uneasy male dignity to defend; who took them as he found them and was completely unselfconscious. There is no act, no sermon, no parable in the whole Gospel that borrows its pungency from female perversity; nobody could possibly guess from the words and deeds of Jesus that there was anything "funny" about woman's nature.[33]

Jesus honoured women. He didn't think there was something "odd" or "difficult" about them. He treated them with respect; he took them seriously, held them responsible and called them to discipleship, just as much as men. Of course, the men in the Gospels had never known a man like Jesus either—who didn't compete with them, put them down, or seek their respect. But it was Jesus' treatment of women that was most noticeably countercultural. This fed into the approach of the early church. Christianity was popular among women in the 1st and 2nd centuries because it offered them so much: the church was for monogamous marriages, which included rights for the wife; it stood against sexual immorality and easy divorce, against abortion and infanticide (often perpetrated against female babies), and against viewing children as disposable sex objects. It encouraged women to learn and be involved in many ministries. For all these reasons and more, Christianity was very pro-women—as it still is!

We must begin by recognising that there is an issue to contend with here. If you are a man, and especially if you are a church leader of any kind, have you seriously contemplated what it might feel like for a woman to think that God prefers men—or at least to suspect that he might? To wonder what it would be like if your life as a disciple of Jesus was counted as "less" simply because of your sex? I (Graham) admit that until recently, I hadn't considered those questions, and it is very sobering to do so. I need to realise that it *does* feel like that, to some women—and that I could even say and do things that might *make* it feel like that.

Acts 16 provides a lovely counterexample for men in ministry. Paul and his companions preach the gospel in Philippi to a group of women at a riverside gathering for prayer (v 13); this sort of group existed when there weren't enough men to form a synagogue. A businesswoman called

Lydia responds to the gospel and believes; she then invites Paul and the others to stay at her house. Notice her reasoning:

"If you consider me a believer in the Lord," she said, "come and stay at my house." And she persuaded us. (Acts 16:15)

Paul doesn't distance himself from this woman; if she is converted, she is a sister in Christ, and they should receive her hospitality. Before long, the new church in Philippi becomes centred on Lydia's house (v 40). There is no suspicion of Lydia as a woman. Instead she is embraced as a fellow disciple and as a patron of the new church.

All this is readily affirmed by evangelicals and rightly so. But does it flow out in practice?

For instance, take the principle that women should learn from Jesus just as much as men. But when setting up a theology reading group at a church, who is invited? What are the topics on the agenda at men's and women's groups? Are women's conferences aimed at "lighter" areas or serious teaching? Who do we consider for deeper theological education?

Or take the principle that women are called to serve Jesus in the church (in whatever capacity we think is appropriate). Hopefully you already have women who serve faithfully, and who may do so more than many men. But what training is given? What acknowledgement is paid? What resources are provided? We must beware in case we subtly show that we think it is only men and their ministry which really counts.

CALLED TO LIFE TOGETHER

Some discussions over gender have tried to produce definitions of masculinity and femininity. We appreciate the desire to specify that, but it's very difficult to do in practice—such definitions almost always tend to over- or underemphasise our similarities or differences. Whereas God, in his wisdom, has not given us a dictionary entry but painted a picture: a common picture of godliness and discipleship that isn't one thing for a man and another for a woman, but is lived and expressed through our two different genders as we seek to follow Jesus together.

That last part is worth emphasising: God calls us to live *together* as men and women. This is something our culture often struggles with. For example, some say that men and women can never "just be friends"; sexual interest will always overtake such a friendship. From a different angle, but with similar results, there is the view that is always suspicious of men. They are regarded as having disqualified themselves from any presumption of innocence through a history of patriarchy and abuse, so they now should not dare to comment on women or attempt to have any meaningful interaction with them unless invited to. These approaches overemphasise differences between us.

We should recognise that traditional Western culture casts a shadow of sexism which still lingers. It's easy to look to the generations older than us and think that they got male/ female relationships wrong but assume that our generation has moved on. In speaking on this topic, I (Graham) was once asked, "Don't you think this is an issue for your age group?" I'm in my early 50s, and for this comparatively young questioner, that put me on the wrong side of progressive thinking. The implication was that while I probably needed to think through my sexism, he didn't. I replied that I had thought exactly the same as him when I was his age. I had looked at older men and presumed that they had sexist attitudes but that I had escaped such outdated ideas. Now I was being looked at in the same way. Presumably this young man too would have a similar moment in years to come.

Our society has become more equal in some ways, but sexism continues. One reason is that—as we saw in chapter 2—we're not just influenced by our background

EMBRACING COMPLEMENTARIANISM

and culture; we're also influenced by our sin. Sin in the male heart can easily show itself in thinking less of, demeaning or objectifying women—and women will show a variety of sinful things in their view of men.

So how do we move forward? By the gospel. The gospel teaches us to admit our sin, to ask for and receive *forgiveness*, and to live in *humility, respect,* and *generosity* with each other.

Consider *humility*. This means we must be willing to consider that we get things wrong. One of the first things to do is to ask questions and listen to the answers.

At Graham's church we conducted a review for women. We wanted to dig into how we were doing in living together. One of the questions we asked was "Do you feel valued, loved, and respected as a woman in this church?" Wonderfully, the majority of women said they did; but there were many helpful comments in addition. These highlighted the way women might be spoken of, who was asked to do different tasks, the way women's voices were heard (or not), and the predominant culture of the church. In all these areas there were blind spots, and we needed to ask the question to become aware of them.

Consider *respect*. This will mean dealing with each person and their concerns, questions, suggestions and issues equally seriously. Specifically, it means neither dismissing nor pandering to anyone because of their sex. It will mean equality of treatment for volunteers and staff in supervision, attention, pay, and more. I know one church, for example, that had a female member of the pastoral staff who didn't have a pension as part of her employment package, but all the male members of staff did. I don't know how that came about, but it was terrible that it did.

Consider *generosity*. This will mean not thinking the worst of people when they might express themselves poorly. It will mean charitably recognising the influences that will have shaped people (while not excusing them), and patiently giving people time to recognise the issues rather than jumping on them for getting it wrong. In being generous, we won't follow the instincts of a "cancel" culture, where, if you make one mistake, you're ruled out of bounds.

Consider *forgiveness*. The author Douglas Murray writes of how, in the online world, people have to live with any past mistakes, which are never erased and can constantly be held over you. He points out how we all tend to make allowances for the people we like and whose views we agree with, but not for those we don't. The result is an even more embedded tribalism. Unfortunately, such tendencies are found in Christian interactions online and in church. Even as an atheist, Murray sees that the only way we can move forward is by forgiveness[34]—how much more should we say that in the church! In a gospel community where people own their gendered sin, they should be freely and fully forgiven; and even where they remain blind to it, we are to "bear with each other" (Colossians 3:13).

Humility, respect, generosity and forgiveness start to describe a community shaped by the gospel—which is very different to how communities in the world are shaped. It's a community that welcomes people despite differences rather than because of similarities. It's a community where people bear with each other's faults, rather than fracturing because of friction. It's a community where men and women can be themselves, confident in their identity as children of God and as brothers and sisters together. It's a community where we can flourish in and through our respective genders rather than denying them or dividing over them. It's a community called the church.

REFLECTION QUESTIONS

For individuals

1. Which of the two dangers (over- or underemphasising difference) might you lean towards?
2. What is helpful and reassuring about being called to godliness rather than gender?
3. Can you think of examples of how you express godliness through your gender?
4. What is encouraging about Jesus' call to discipleship?
5. Which of the attitudes on pages 65-66 do you want to develop so as to live life well together with others?

For a group

1. Which of the two dangers (over- or underemphasising difference) might our church lean towards?
2. Do we appropriately call people to godliness rather than gender?
3. Share examples of where you see people being godly in different ways and so expressing their gender.
4. How well are we doing in heeding God's call to life together?
5. What attitudes might we need to grow in to live life well together?

5.

The Goodness of Men
Leading in Ministry

I (Jane) am surrounded by many capable Christian women. Isobel oversees a conference that thousands of women attend each year. Kellie is a missionary in Japan. Susanna is involved in Bible translation. Kara is archdeacon for women's ministry in her diocese. Claire is a New Testament scholar. Tara has helped train hundreds of people for various ministries. These women are clearly gifted, and the kingdom of God has been extended through them. In fact, the history of God's people is full of countless examples of gifted female leaders. So, if women are so capable and so much good comes from their ministries, why restrict their role at all?

While complementarians have different views on which roles in church life are inappropriate for women, the common starting point is that the role of church leader—such as elder or pastor—is reserved for qualified men only. Even this "basic" prohibition has come under much scrutiny in recent years. It can seem to go against logic, experience, calling and gifting, and justice itself. Some believe the refusal to admit women as elders impedes evangelism and edification. They might argue that while God accommodated his message to the patriarchal cultures into which it was originally written, ultimately he disapproved of it, and now that society has become more equal, the church too should move beyond any restrictions on female leadership in the home, church, or society more generally.[35]

Given the mounting pressure from our society, and within certain sections of the church, for women to be church leaders, why would we continue to maintain that only certain *men* are fit for this office? Can such a pattern really be embraced as a good thing?

THE GOOD GIFT OF LEADERS

When writing to the Ephesian church, Paul does not describe Christian leadership structures as simply emerging from within a particular culture. Instead, he writes of what *Christ did.* Christ, having conquered death, then ascended triumphantly to heaven, from where he gave gifts to his church (Ephesians 4:8-12). And the surprise twist is that these gifts are *people*— people occupying key roles of leadership (v 11). These originally included the apostles, the prophets, the evangelists, and the pastors (shepherds) and teachers. They were given to equip God's people, so that the church as a whole would be built up and God's saving gospel would go out from them.[36]

Complementarians have different views as to how many of these roles continue to operate in the church today and which were unique to the New Testament era. However, the relevant point for us at this point is twofold. First, leaders in the church are a gift from Jesus—so he, rather than the people concerned themselves or the culture in which they operate, determines who is appropriate to exercise these ministries. Second, leaders in the church are a *good* gift. Jesus gives leaders in the way that he does for the growth and maturing of his body; they are good, and they are for our good. That should shape the way we approach this. Too often today leadership is seen as a necessary evil; Jesus thinks it's a good gift we need for our growth.

So what should church leadership look like? We see examples of leadership across the New Testament: for example, Paul and Barnabas appointing elders in new churches (Acts 14:23). But we hear more specific instructions in Paul's letters to Timothy and Titus, who were responsible for organising churches. Paul says to Timothy that he is writing to him so that…

> … *you will know how people ought to conduct themselves in God's household, which is the church of the living God, the pillar and foundation of the truth. (1 Timothy 3:15)*

Paul goes on to discuss two clear positions in church life: elders and deacons. The word "overseer" is also used, and some suggest this refers to a third office; however, there are good reasons to take elder, overseer, and pastor as titles for the same people and function (see Acts 20:17, 28-29; 1 Timothy 3:1, 8; Titus 1:5-9; Philippians 1:1).

THE GOOD CHARACTER OF LEADERS

For both elders and deacons, what is of overwhelming importance is their godly character and sound convictions, rather than their ability or capacity. This is made abundantly clear in the criteria Paul gives in 1 Timothy 3:1-13 and Titus 1:5-9. It then flows out in the descriptions of what the leaders are to do. For example, elders are to be "gentle" in character, and this means that when opposed, they "gently instruct" their opponents (2 Timothy 2:24-26). In fact, the elder's teaching ability is not simply a skill but something intimately connected to this character and conviction (Titus 1:9).

We see this same emphasis in Peter's exhortation to elders:

> *Be shepherds of God's flock that is under your care, watching over them—not because you must, but because you are willing, as God wants you to be; not pursuing*

*dishonest gain, but eager to serve; not lording it over those
entrusted to you, but being examples to the flock.*

(1 Peter 5:2-3)

In the end, it's all about character. As Robert Murray
M'Cheyne reportedly said, "The greatest need of my people
is my personal holiness".

WHAT ELDERS DO

Before coming to the question of whether women can be
elders, let's consider the role itself. (We'll return to deacons
later.) We've seen that they are to be good examples and to
serve those they care for. They are also "overseers", who are to
"oversee" the church: that is, they are to look out for people's
safety and protection, and are responsible for their welfare
and growth. They are shepherds, who are to "shepherd" the
flock. The picture of shepherd combines elements of feeding,
caring, protecting and nurturing; it includes seeking the strays
and binding up the injured (see Ezekiel 34:4). They are to act
for the good of the flock, who have been entrusted to them
by God (Acts 20:28).

A prime way they do this is in teaching. They must be able
to teach (1 Timothy 3:2) and will devote themselves to "the
public reading of Scripture, preaching and teaching" (4:13).
This teaching will often have a "positive" and a "negative" side
to it: they are to "encourage others by sound doctrine and
refute those who oppose it" (Titus 1:9).

But elders are more than just "instructors"; they lead the life
of the church. That's why Paul says that an overseer…

*… must manage his own family well and see that his
children obey him, and he must do so in a manner worthy
of full respect. (If anyone does not know how to manage his
own family, how can he take care of God's church?)*

(1 Timothy 3:4-5)

Managing the church family means taking responsibility for its whole life, being concerned for its health and growth, caring for its members and getting involved in its relationships. That's the holistic picture of leadership given in the New Testament.

There are many concerns expressed about leadership and authority in the church—and rightly so, because they can be grossly misused. The answer to poor leadership in the Bible isn't "no leadership"; it's good leadership, under God. We need to keep holding on to the goodness of leaders of good character.

THE GOOD LEADERSHIP OF MEN

Let's return to the question of women in church leadership. What's clear is that there is no indication in the New Testament that women were appointed elders of churches. Women are *capable* of what is required of elders, such as being in right standing with God and people; of having a consistent life; of loving and serving those under their care; and of teaching what is sound doctrine and warning others against false doctrine. These are things we would expect of many mature Christian women (and men). But we do not see women doing this in the *context* of the office of elder.

The key passage here is in 1 Timothy 2:

> *Let a woman learn quietly with all submissiveness. I do not permit a woman to teach or to exercise authority over a man; rather, she is to remain quiet. For Adam was formed first, then Eve; and Adam was not deceived, but the woman was deceived and became a transgressor.*
>
> *(1 Timothy 2:11-14, ESV)*

This instruction comes as part of a discussion about public worship or the formal gathering of the church. And in this context, Paul says women are to learn in quietness and submission, and that they are not to teach or have authority over a man. Notice how quietness and submission are set in contrast to teaching and authority. The call to be quiet does not mean a woman never speaks in church. (The word used doesn't mean "silence".) Rather, she is quiet when the teaching is happening; she is receiving it rather than giving it. It also does not, in our view, mean that women are to submit to all men: "Rather, women are to be submissive *in* church, *when* the teaching is happening, *to* what is taught and those men who are teaching it." [37]

The right understanding of these verses is greatly debated and can get very involved. Some interpreters argue that what looks like a restriction on the role of women here either wasn't that originally or that it was but it no longer applies now. These arguments turn on understanding what was happening in Ephesus at the time (where Timothy was), how much Paul accommodated his message to the culture, the meaning of specific words, and more. A number of books deal with these questions in depth.[38] Here, though, we will focus on what we think Paul *did* mean, rather than describing all the possible interpretations.

It is important to note, first, that Paul is not restricting women from all types of teaching. Paul commands women elsewhere to teach (see Titus 2:3); he had female co-workers who shared God's word with others (for example, Priscilla, Acts 18:18-28; and see Romans 16:3); he spoke about women prophesying (1 Corinthians 11:5); and women are encouraged to teach and instruct in the "one another" commands given to all Christians (see Colossians 3:16). We will return to these areas in the next chapters. Yet, despite all the occasions on which Paul encourages women to teach, here in 1 Timothy 2:12 he imposes a prohibition. So, what does Paul have in mind?

To answer that question, we need to consider how the "teaching" and the "authority" that Paul refers to relate to each other. The way Paul writes this shows that these two ideas are identifiable but closely connected. By way of comparison, the same type of phrasing is used in Jesus' words about heaven as a place where "thieves do not break in and steal" (Matthew 6:20). "Breaking in" and "stealing" are identifiably different actions (you break the window, and then you take something); but they are used in this closely connected way to refer to one overall action. So here, the teaching and authority go hand in hand; this is referring to teaching in a way that exercises authority within the church.

This fits with the context of 1 Timothy; it makes sense that the teaching in view in 2:12 is the authoritative teaching of the elders, who were to defend the truth against the false teaching that was clearly circulating in Ephesus (see 1:3-4). This is where our chapter divisions are potentially unhelpful, as in chapter 3 Paul immediately goes on to talk about overseers or elders, who must be able to teach (3:2). This teaching is the public tradition about Christ and the Scriptures (2:7; 2 Timothy 3:16; 4:2; Titus 2:7; James 3:1). Teaching this was something which Timothy clearly did (1 Timothy 4:11-16) and which the elders were to do too (5:17).

So, if you were explaining the meaning and implications of 1 Timothy 2:11-12 to a friend, you could say, "If a woman teaches as an elder, then logically she has authority over men in the church, and Paul does not permit this. Rather, a woman should learn from an elder's authoritative teaching in the gathered assembly in quietness and full submission."

This means we need to distinguish between the authoritative teaching of the elders and the mutual "one another" teaching that everyone is to do in the church. This has been helpfully labelled by the writer Andrew Wilson as capital "T" Teaching and lowercase "t" teaching.[39] Everyone is to do "teaching", but only men who have the role of elder are to do "Teaching".

We will explore how this applies in church life more fully in a later chapter, but it's worth anticipating a few issues. Some complementarians, including Wilson, believe that this means that women should not be appointed as elders, but that they can do all forms of teaching, including public preaching, so long as it is done under the authority of the elders. Whether or not this is the case comes down to the question of how preaching functions in the life of the church. So, while this is an understandable position, our own view would be that preaching in the weekly gathering is usually an exercise of authority by virtue of its nature and place in the church. (It is, in other words, "Big 'T' Teaching".) If so, that means that such preaching is inappropriate from women. (There is more discussion on this point and about who should preach in Appendix 1.)

As mentioned above, some people argue that Paul's prohibition about women teaching was given in the context of that church and has no ongoing significance for us today. Perhaps it was that 1st-century women were uneducated, and so they needed to focus on learning first; or that the Artemis cult in Ephesus unduly elevated the role of women. But Paul's argument is clearly based on creation and the fall: Adam was created first (v 13), and Eve was the one who was deceived (v 14). The Genesis narrative is essential to Paul's understanding of who we are as men and women more generally. Adam and Eve were not just any ordinary couple in history. There is an order between men and women that was shown in the first marriage and rejected in the fall, and which Paul now applies to the organisation of the household of God. So Paul has not just randomly picked stories from Genesis 2 and 3 to apply to the church at Ephesus. Rather, what happened in Genesis gives the reason why the church of God, not just the church in Ephesus, is ordered the way it is.[40]

LEADERSHIP IN 1 CORINTHIANS 11 AND 14

There are two other key passages that point us to the good leadership of men within the church. They are both in 1 Corinthians and are also greatly contested.

In 1 Corinthians 11, Paul discusses how men and women speak in the church. He says:

> *² I praise you for remembering me in everything and for holding to the traditions just as I passed them on to you. ³But I want you to realise that the head of every man is Christ, and the head of the woman is man, and the head of Christ is God. ⁴ Every man who prays or prophesies with his head covered dishonours his head. ⁵ But every woman who prays or prophesies with her head uncovered dishonours her head—it is the same as having her head shaved. ⁶ For if a woman does not cover her head, she might as well have her hair cut off; but if it is a disgrace for a woman to have her hair cut off or her head shaved, then she should cover her head.*
>
> *⁷ A man ought not to cover his head, since he is the image and glory of God; but woman is the glory of man. ⁸ For man did not come from woman, but woman from man; ⁹ neither was man created for woman, but woman for man. ¹⁰ It is for this reason that a woman ought to have authority over her own head, because of the angels. ¹¹ Nevertheless, in the Lord woman is not independent of man, nor is man independent of woman. ¹² For as woman came from man, so also man is born of woman. But everything comes from God. (1 Corinthians 11:1-12)*

Paul makes clear that when the church is gathered, the differences between males and females are to be obvious physically, such as in the way they dress and their hairstyles. The ministry that men and women can do is in one respect the same, in that they both can pray and prophesy. But they are to do these ministries as a man or as a woman. Paul gives three key reasons for the differences between men and women—reasons which, as in 1 Timothy 2, hark back to the Genesis narrative and therefore transcend time and culture (v 3, v 8-10, v 11-12). The bottom line is that our gender matters. To not look as your sex brings shame upon your head (v 4-6) and results in disordered relationships. When both men and women look like their gender, this brings glory to God. Although clothing and head coverings will vary from culture to culture, anybody can normally go anywhere in the world and tell straight away who is female and who is male. It is only in more recent times that a blurring of sexual differences is becoming more accepted in some societies. But this is a dangerous rejection of who we actually are. This passage, along with 1 Timothy 2:8-15 and Ephesians 5:21-33, teach us that the two human sexes model to us greater realities—the relationship between God and us, and the relationship between Christ and his church.[41]

Three chapters later, in 1 Corinthians 14, Paul again mentions prophecy, commending it as a ministry that is to be very much desired for men and women (v 5). Exactly what is meant by the word "prophecy" in the New Testament is, again, much debated. It appears not to have been the same as Old Testament prophecy, primarily because New Testament prophecies were to be weighed (v 29), whereas Old Testament prophecies came simply as "the word of the Lord". Our own view is that New Testament prophecy seems to have been a testimony, or an application of, or response to God's word, since we are told that people were instructed and encouraged by it (v 31). As with praying and singing, there was a place for prophecy in the public gathering—it was not something merely done privately or in a one to one setting (v 26; also 11:5).

Given that, verse 34 may come as a shock:

Women should remain silent in the churches. They are not
allowed to speak, but must be in submission, as the law says.

How are we to understand this prohibition? As with
1 Timothy 2, Paul can't mean that women never speak when
the church gathers. Not only has he already mentioned
their praying and prophesying in chapter 11, but earlier in
chapter 14 he lists ways in which everyone might contribute
in speech:

> *What then shall we say, brothers and sisters? When you*
> *come together, each of you has a hymn, or a word of*
> *instruction, a revelation, a tongue or an interpretation.*
> *Everything must be done so that the church may be built*
> *up. (1 Corinthians 14:26)*

This is not an exhaustive list (there's no mention of prayer,
for instance). But many things can be said when they gather!
Paul reiterates the governing principle that decides whether
something should happen in their gathering: everything
should build up the church. This principle is then applied in
verses 27-35. For each gift he states a limit, he gives reasons
for the restrictions, and he insists on silence in some parts of
the church. For example, if there is no interpreter, the person
speaking in tongues should keep quiet (v 28). If someone
else gets a revelation, the person prophesying should stop
(v 29). So it is not just women who are told to keep quiet
under certain circumstances! And the aim is good order in the
church so that people can be built up.

Given the context, and the expectation in chapter 11 that
women will prophesy, it appears that the specific circumstance
Paul has in view in verses 34-35 is the weighing of prophecies.
In this situation women are to be silent, but they can be
involved in the weighing of prophecy by asking their "men"
when they are at home (v 35). This might not be limited

to wives and husbands, but involve men and women more generally in the household.[42]

So we've seen that while women contribute in many ways within public worship, there are also restrictions. The reasons for these go back to creation; they are not simply cultural, even if some of them are then expressed in cultural ways (such as clothing or hairstyles). We still need to then go through the process of "mapping" these restrictions onto church life today, which we will look at in a later chapter.

WHAT ABOUT DEACONS?

We said earlier that there were two clear "offices" described in the New Testament church: elders and deacons. We've majored on elders because they are the group we know most about and seem to be the clear overall leaders in the church.[43] But deacons are also mentioned (for example, Philippians 1:1), and Paul specifies qualifications for that role in 1 Timothy 3:8-13.

There is some debate on what exactly deacons do because we're never explicitly told. Deacons are expected to be very similar to elders in terms of their character and conviction, but it is notable that an ability to teach is required of elders but not of deacons (1 Timothy 3:2). Some churches and denominations work off the pattern we see in Acts 6, where the apostles hand over responsibility for food distribution to others. This is usually taken to mean that elders are to be primarily concerned with word ministry and deacons are to be mainly involved in ministries of mercy—although that is not to say that elders are never involved in ministries of mercy or that deacons never teach (as Stephen and Philip do in Acts).

The word deacon simply means "servant", and so one way to think about them is as officially recognised servants within the community of the church. They often take responsibility for more practical areas of church life such as finance, buildings, or legal matters. But we don't feel they need to be restricted to such areas.

Complementarians take different views on whether women can be deacons. This turns on two points: first, whether 1 Timothy 3 refers to female deacons or not, and second, what those who are called "deacons" actually do in the life of the church.

Regarding the first point: in 1 Timothy 3:11, there are requirements as to what a certain group of women should be like. Some take this as referring to female deacons, whereas others take it to be referring to deacons' wives.[44] Both complementarians and egalitarians can be found on each side of this particular debate. However, whether Paul is speaking about female deacons or deacon's wives, it is not surprising that once again his focus is on character driven by conviction: "In the same way, the women are to be worthy of respect, not malicious talkers but temperate and trustworthy in everything".

If Paul is referring to female deacons, then clearly women can serve in this way! But even if you conclude that he's referring to wives here, you may still decide that women can serve as deacons, if the area of service assigned to deacons in your church doesn't involve the authoritative teaching that we looked at earlier. Others would argue that a deacon's status as part of the church's official leadership means that women should not have this role. Some of this will also depend on your church's understanding of what a "deacon" is and does.[45]

WHERE NEXT?

We've seen that leadership is a good gift from Christ to his people, and that such leadership is expressed in teaching and authority in the life of the church. We've seen that this "authoritative teaching" or overall church leadership is limited to qualified men. We've started to see that there are other forms of ministry (such as prophecy, prayer, singing, encouragement and more) which everyone—men and women—contribute to. In the future chapters we will consider these wider aspects of ministry more specifically, including examples of what women can do "up front", before stepping back to consider what these should look like in our churches.

REFLECTION QUESTIONS

For individuals

1. How do you feel about leadership? What difference does it make that Jesus gives leaders as his gift to the church?
2. How is the character of leaders foundational to their role?
3. What do you make of the restriction of overall leadership to men?
4. Do you, or could you, think of this as a good thing?
5. What role do you think deacons have in the church?

For a group

1. How does your church regard leadership? Is it a necessary evil or a good gift?
2. What are seen as the primary qualifications for leaders in your church? Where is character rated?
3. How does your church understand the restriction of overall leadership to men?
4. Is that embraced or are people embarrassed about it?
5. What role do deacons have in your church?

6.
Understanding Church

My (Graham's) wife has worked for a wide range of organisations over the years—each of which have had different cultures and "feels" to them. The entrepreneurial start-up company feels different to the established organisation. The image-conscious branding group feels different to the relational Christian charity. Doing the same type of work feels different in those different settings because it is shaped by the context.

So how should church feel? What "shaping" influence should it have?

That is crucial to consider because the local church is the context for all our life and ministry. Our understanding of it will shape everything that happens in it and in us. Many discussions of complementarianism have assumed an understanding of the church, or at worst, ignored it. This is where we need to understand the identity of the church (who we are) before we answer questions about the life of the church (what we do).

Identity of the church ⟶ Life of the church

The identity of the church leads to the life of the church. In discussing church life, whether with regard to complementarianism or any other topic, we often begin on the right-hand side of the diagram. We start with functions and practicalities: what do we do as church? We can list various activities: teaching, discipling, evangelising, praying, praising. The question is then: what's the best way to do those? And which parts should women do?

Instead, let's start with the left-hand side. The questions we need to ask first are: who are we and what are we, and so how should we live together?

THE IDENTITY OF THE CHURCH

Ephesians 2:11-22 is key to answering the question "Who are we as a church?" Paul starts in verses 11-12 by talking about how the Gentiles were not part of the people of God in the Old Testament (the Jews)—they were "excluded" (v 12). But then he moves to the change brought about by Jesus: "But now in Christ Jesus you who once were far away have been brought near by the blood of Christ" (v 13). Through Jesus' death the Gentiles have been brought close to God.

But that also means a change in their relationship with Jewish followers of Christ. There used to be a barrier between these two groups—a "dividing wall of hostility" (v 14). That barrier has been destroyed by Jesus so that they can be at peace and be united. Paul sums up Jesus' purpose in verse 15:

His purpose was to create in himself one new humanity out of the two, thus making peace. (Ephesians 2:15)

This is an amazing statement. If I were to ask you, "Why did Jesus die?" you rightly answer, "To reconcile us to God". But from this verse we should also answer, "To bring peace between people". In fact, not just to bring peace but to create *a new humanity* who are at peace. Jesus takes these two groups, bitterly divided, and he creates a new breed of human in himself, where they are united.

In British rugby, nations like England and Wales usually play against each other—and do so in fierce competition. Scotland refers to England as the "old enemy". But once every four years the British and Irish Lions team is formed, which is made up of players from England, Wales, Scotland and Ireland. When that happens, players who have been on opposing sides become teammates. They take off their national colours and put on a new shirt. That new identity means they are united.

So it is in the church. The deep divides between Jew and Gentile are overcome through the work of Christ, as Paul says to the Galatians:

> *There is neither Jew nor Gentile, neither slave nor free, nor is there male and female, for you are all one in Christ Jesus.*
> *(Galatians 3:28)*

Paul here refers to three deep social divides in the 1st century: between Jew and Gentile, slave and free, and male and female. These social realities created barriers between each group and that shaped interactions between them. Jews and Gentiles wouldn't eat together. A Jewish man often prayed a threefold thanksgiving in which he thanked God that he had not made him a Gentile, a slave or a female.

So it is utterly remarkable for Paul to say that in Christ, "there is neither..." or that "you are all one in Christ Jesus". There is a unity between anyone and everyone who is in Christ, which is based on our identity in Christ. What is most important about us now is not our gender, ethnicity, or social status—it's being in Jesus.

Of course, people who were in Jesus would remain male or female, Jewish or Gentile, slave or free (although that latter distinction could change). Becoming a Christian does not eliminate such differences. But it does eliminate the *divisions* caused by those differences. Previously there was a separation, antagonism and superiority/inferiority. Now there is equality, unity and togetherness. Rather than saying, "I'm glad I'm not like you", we say, "You are like me".

This is the basis for the church—Jesus gives us a new identity and a new set of relationships is brought into being. So, Paul goes on to say in Ephesians 2, every believer, whether Jew or Gentile, is now a citizen in God's nation, a member of God's household and part of God's temple (v 19-22). We have a new corporate identity together.

This is very different to thinking that trusting in Jesus only changes my relationship with God. We easily think only in terms of a "vertical" change, in being forgiven and adopted by God, rather than this "horizontal" change, by which I am united with other people. If we only think in vertical terms, then that shapes our approach to church life: church is all about helping me in my new relationship with God. Other people in church life are useful in as much as they help me in that relationship.

If that is what church is, then leaders will simply ask, "What are the most efficient ways of helping everyone in their new relationship with God?" But if there is a horizontal change, then we have a new relationship to live out with other people. Now we ask, "How should we live as God's people together?"

THE LIFE OF THE CHURCH

The identity of the church leads to the life of the church. Let's consider different aspects of that life.

Unity

Paul goes on later in Ephesians like this:

> *Be completely humble and gentle; be patient, bearing with one another in love. Make every effort to keep the unity of the Spirit through the bond of peace. (Ephesians 4:2-3)*

The unity and oneness that Jesus has created needs to be lived out and preserved. It's interesting to ask what sort of relationships Paul is picturing in the church. He's clearly thinking that church life is relationally close enough to require these attitudes—where there is enough interaction that we would need to be patient and bear with or forgive one another (see also Colossians 3:13). He's not picturing a group that simply sit in the same building for an hour once a week and that's it.

Paul is also expecting unity between a variety of people. That mix of Jews/Gentiles, slaves/free and men/women is precisely what requires attitudes of gentleness and humility. Living alongside people who are different to us is not easy! What Paul doesn't say is, "Why not organise yourselves to make things run more smoothly?" He could have said that slaves work longer hours and are less well-educated, so let's have a later service for them, and the free people can meet earlier. Or he could have said that Jews and Gentiles eating together is really awkward, so let's just split into two groups. Or that men and women are used to being divided in the Jewish temple, so let's divide them in the church.

It would have been easier to divide in those ways, and it may have been more efficient, but it would have been a betrayal of their new identity. This is really significant in regards to the tendency in some churches today to have separate streams of ministry for men and women. While there may be a good place for that, it should only ever be an addition to normal church life, where men and women live life together.

Equality

This understanding of unity has significance for how we think and speak about equality. Complementarians rightly speak of equality between men and women in their dignity and worth. As we've seen, we are created equally in the image of God, we are equally heirs in the gift of life (1 Peter 3:7), and we are equally part of the body of Christ (1 Corinthians 12:6, 7, 11, 13, 18, 27). So in the church, no one is more "in" than anyone else, no one is more precious to God than anyone else, and no one is more important than anyone else. We believe in equality.

That language of equality is right in what it affirms, but it doesn't go far enough in describing the nature of this new community. Equality in our culture tends to emphasise individuals: "How am I treated? What can I do? What is my place?" But the focus in Ephesians is not on individual equality but on a new corporate identity:

> *Consequently, you are no longer foreigners and strangers, but fellow citizens with God's people and also members of his household, built on the foundation of the apostles and prophets, with Christ Jesus himself as the chief cornerstone. In him the whole building is joined together and rises to become a holy temple in the Lord. And in him you too are being built together to become a dwelling in which God lives by his Spirit. (Ephesians 2:19-22)*

> *There is one body and one Spirit, just as you were called to one hope when you were called; one Lord, one faith, one baptism; one God and Father of all, who is over all and through all and in all. (Ephesians 4:4-6)*

We're not simply all equal—we're one. We're called not just to assert equality between ourselves but to embrace a corporate identity. What difference would it make to our churches if we were more concerned about what happened among us as a whole than what we got to do individually? If our greater concern was for the whole?

For those of us living in more individualistic cultures, the way in which we contest limits on the roles of women in the church can sometimes reveal a worldly way of thinking about equality that focuses on individuals, not on the whole. Instead, we should want to celebrate who are we *together*: that God dwells among *us* as his new temple and that *we* are the body of Christ.

That picture of the body teaches us both that we are all equally part of the body no matter what our differences are and should be treated as such, *and* that we all form a new whole.

Growth

Paul speaks in Ephesians 4 of the growth of the church:

> *So Christ himself gave the apostles, the prophets, the evangelists, the pastors and teachers, to equip his people for works of service, so that the body of Christ may be built up until we all reach unity in the faith and in the knowledge of the Son of God and become mature, attaining to the whole measure of the fullness of Christ. (Ephesians 4:11-13)*

Consider the picture of growth and maturity that Paul gives. It is growth as a body, not as individuals. *We all* grow, and the end point of growth is that we "become in every respect the mature body of him who is the head, that is, Christ" (v 15). So what Paul is describing is not individual Christ-likeness in each person; it is maturity as a whole group.

Think of a team sport, like football, where an individual can grow in their abilities and skills. You can say that the individual is growing as a player. But you can also talk of how a team grows and matures in playing *as a team*. And in a team sport, individual skill is only meaningful if it contributes to the whole team. Being a great individual player doesn't mean anything by itself.

Church is a team sport. And church growth is growth as a *team*. Maturity is shown in how the whole church works within itself; how people treat each other; how people think about each other; how they hold on to the truth together. You can only see if a church is growing by looking at the quality of relationships.

Our default is to think of growth in individualistic terms. And while we *can* ask the question of how individuals are doing, the answer should always be connected to how they are operating in church. To put it differently, we're not after a Christian version of individual "self-realisation". Our culture encourages people to "be who you are" and "be all you can be". The Christian version just adds God: "Be all God wants you to be". While there is some merit in that, it only encourages us to think individually. Whereas in the church, our desire should be to be who we all are together in Christ, and all that he wants us to be. We want to realise our corporate identity.

This vision of growth will play out in church life in many ways. It will mean that we are not concerned simply with efficient ways of teaching people but with relationships. We'll see the ministry of the whole body as being needed for the growth of the whole body (an idea we'll return to in the next chapter). While church leaders play a key role in this, it's more like directing an orchestra in playing well together as an orchestra—rather than simply giving individual music lessons.

Family

When Paul wrote to Timothy to tell him how people should live in the church, he summed up the purpose of his instructions like this:

> *Although I hope to come to you soon, I am writing to you with these instructions so that, if I am delayed, you will know how people ought to conduct themselves in God's household, which is the church of the living God, the pillar and foundation of the truth. (1 Timothy 3:14-15)*

We see here the identity of church: it is God's household or family, which is also the pillar and foundation of the truth. That identity then leads to a way of conducting life within the church ("how people ought to conduct themselves"). Much of 1 Timothy describes that life: who should be leaders, how widows should be cared for, how error is to be dealt with, and so on. It is the life of a family that is shaped by God's truth.

Paul repeats that family picture in speaking of how Timothy, as a young pastor, should relate to different groups in the church:

> *Do not rebuke an older man harshly, but exhort him as if he were your father. Treat younger men as brothers, older women as mothers, and younger women as sisters, with absolute purity. (1 Timothy 5:1-2)*

Essentially Paul is saying, *Treat people in church as family members*. We can extend that model from Timothy to each of us; we think of others as fathers, mothers, brothers and sisters, depending on the combination of gender, age, and stage of life between us.

That family picture gives us a number of ingredients that should be found in church relationships. There is love and warmth and closeness. This is family, so we're not dispassionate, professional or distanced. But there is also respect. I think of an older woman as a mother, and so I respect her, value her opinions and contribution, and am glad for her service and care. There's a lovely phrase that Paul uses in Romans 16, where he says that the mother of Rufus "has been a mother to me, too" (Romans 16:13); he respected and valued her. I think of others as brothers in the faith and so value their companionship and encouragement. I think of some as daughters and so want to care for and protect them, nurture them and encourage them; I don't want to be patronising or dismissive.

Relationships also need to be appropriate: Paul has to add "with absolute purity" because of the potential for relationships to be twisted by sin—most probably sexual sin in this case. There are dangers of these types in relationships, in this case between Timothy as a younger man with younger women. But Paul doesn't say, *Because there are dangers, don't have any relationship with them.* The answer isn't to steer clear of young women; the answer is for there to be appropriate familial relationships, with love, respect, and purity.

So do we think of our church as a family, as opposed to an organisation? Of course, most of us *speak* of church as family. If you were to ask someone if their church is a family, they'd be unlikely to say, "No!" But is that how we relate? Is family the model that actually shapes how we live?

Love

This family picture leads into the love of the church:

> *Follow God's example, therefore, as dearly loved children and walk in the way of love, just as Christ loved us and gave himself up for us as a fragrant offering and sacrifice to God. (Ephesians 5:1-2)*

We love each other in the church because God has loved us. And we model our love for each other on the example Jesus gave of sacrificial love. "In view of God's mercy," we are to "be devoted to another in love" (Romans 12:1, 10). The word for "love" here is "brotherly love" (*philadelphia*)—sibling or family love. We are to be devoted to one another in that sort of love because we're family. The command to love is one of the most common in the New Testament, and it leads into related "one another" commands: to care for each other, to carry each other's burdens, to serve one another, to accept one another, to be patient with one another, and more.

So the quality of church is shown in the quality of relationships. Of course, we want quality in every area of church: quality teaching, quality services, quality kids' work. But having high-quality meetings is not the sign of a quality church. There is the danger that a church could have good services and even good ministry but poor relationships—good structures and activities but poor family life.

What we regard as "quality church life" will shape what we expect from its leaders. As we saw in chapter 5, elders are the "head of the household", who take overall responsibility for the teaching, instruction and managing of family life so that it is governed by God's word and grows in these ways. That will mean that the elders will have a particular concern for anyone who is more vulnerable or weak in the family. They are shepherds, who lovingly seek out the wandering sheep, bind up the injured, strengthen the weak and protect the flock from wolves (see Ezekiel 34:1-16). It's not that they are the only ones doing this—as we've seen, everyone is involved. But they are overseeing it and making sure it happens. Contrast that picture with some traditional views in which caring for vulnerable people is seen as "lesser" ministry that should be done by women. Too often it has been that men teach and women care. That's terrible in many ways!

At one church that I (Jane) was part of, there was a formal pastoral care team. The pastor of the church oversaw this ministry and met with the team once a week to pray for people, to communicate people's particular needs, and to co-ordinate who would visit who, and so on. The team was largely made up of older women. Their availability mid-week in the mornings, and their life and ministry experience, all helped to equip them well for such a ministry, and their insights certainly helped the pastor better care for the flock he was responsible for. Their involvement also meant that he and the other elders were not overwhelmed with doing all the care themselves. It was a great example of men and women—younger and older—serving together for the good of the church family.

Authority
Part of embracing complementarianism is embracing authority and leadership within the life of the church family.

We may find this difficult because our culture often regards authority as a necessary evil at best and a self-centred power play at worst.

We're right to have our suspicions because power can be misused. But the answer is not no authority but a biblical model of authority. Sheep without a shepherd is a bad thing in the Bible! The concept of authority is essential to the Christian life. We believe in the authority of God. We submit to him as Lord. We allow his revelation in his word to guide our thinking, feeling and acting. And he has placed leaders in the church to exercise authority as they bring that word to bear on our lives.

It is right to emphasise how this is a *servant* leadership. Jesus countered his disciples' thinking on power and position by pointing to himself as the one who had come to serve. Rather than following their culture in being those who "lord it over" others, they needed to become "slave of all" (Mark 10:41-45). So, we need leaders who think of themselves as servants more than leaders—but leading is still part of it.

We see this when the apostle Peter echoes Jesus' words in his exhortation to elders:

> *Be shepherds of God's flock that is under your care,*
> *watching over them—not because you must, but because*
> *you are willing, as God wants you to be; not pursuing*
> *dishonest gain, but eager to serve; not lording it over those*
> *entrusted to you, but being examples to the flock.*
>
> *(1 Peter 5:2-3)*

Peter emphasises the willing service of elders, in contrast to "pursuing dishonest gain"; this is a role in which you give rather than get. Likewise, he contrasts "lording it over" people with being an example to them. However, he still sees them as shepherds who watch over the flock who are under their care.

This lands for us in two ways. First, for church members, it means we should appreciate and receive such leadership from suitably qualified men. As Peter goes on to say, "Submit yourselves to your elders" (v 5). This means bowing to how God has organised his church and knowing that it is for our good as a family that we are led in this way. This is how we will be glad of complementarian leadership rather than begrudging it.

Second, for church leaders, it means we should make sure that we are leading the whole family in a way that cares for everyone. We are not to defend our position but expend ourselves for the good of others. We are not to simply give speeches at the family meal table but to care for everyone in the family and get involved in the nitty-gritty of family relationships. We are to lead the whole family into contributing and receiving, and so growing and flourishing as a result. In this way we will help make complementarian leadership attractive.

THE CHURCH AS CONTEXT

Church is the context in which complementarianism gets worked out, and that context has a shaping influence on how complementarianism "feels". You could have two churches which have exactly the same roles for men and women, where they do and don't do the same things; but the *feel* of those churches, and the nature of relationships within them, could be very different. If we want members of our church to embrace complementarianism, then how we think of unity, equality, growth, family, love, and authority matters a great deal.

REFLECTION QUESTIONS

For individuals

1. What difference does it make to thinking about complementarianism to start with the identity of the church rather than its life?
2. What strikes you about the identity of the church described in this chapter?
3. Of the list of descriptions of the life of the church, which ones do you think are most significant for you?
4. How would complementarian ministry feel in a church that was shaped in this way?

For a group

1. Do you think your church tends to start with "identity" as a church or "life" as a church?
2. What would you want to change in the way you and your members think about church?
3. From the list of descriptions of the life of the church, which do you think fits your church well? Which could it grow in?
4. What resulting "feel" does your church have? What difference does that make to complementarian ministry?

7.

Understanding Ministry

What ministry does your church focus on?

Or put another way, what would people in your church think of as the ministry that really counts—the ministry that brings real growth?

Classically in conservative evangelical churches, the answer is preaching, usually as part of a Sunday service. It's true that preaching is essential to the health of a church and has a prime function in facilitating its growth. I (Graham) do it most Sundays!

But if preaching is *the* focus in a church—if that's seen to be *real* ministry, either by design or by default—and if it's something that only men can do, then we give the impression that ministry can only be done by men. If preaching is the ministry that really counts, then ministry done by women is already in second place.

Of course, your church might make something else the focus of ministry. It could be one-to-one discipleship, small groups, missional communities, or the experience of corporate worship. But whatever your focus is, it's bound to have some effect on the role of men and women.

So is there a focus, an exclusiveness, to what really counts as ministry in your church, or is there a breadth? How do different ministries in the church relate to each other? And what is the knock-on effect on men's and women's contributions in the life of the church and how those contributions are seen? As we'll see, we should welcome, appreciate and nurture a wide range of ministry from everyone—including women—because that's how churches grow: "From [Christ] the whole body, joined and held together by every supporting ligament, grows and builds itself up in love, as each part does its work" (Ephesians 4:16).

MINISTRY IN MULTICOLOUR, NOT MONOCHROME

The elders of any congregation (whatever title they have in your church) have a particular role in teaching, in encouraging in sound doctrine and in refuting error (see 1 Timothy 5:17 and Titus 1:9). But it doesn't stop there: the New Testament is full of what are often called the "one another" commands, which are about *mutual ministry*. We are to teach one another, instruct one another, encourage one another, correct each other and speak the truth in love to one another. There are both authoritative teaching roles *and* a one-another mutuality of teaching, in which everyone has a role. While these are distinguishable, there is great overlap—it's not that when the elders are teaching, something completely different is happening from when two people study the Bible together. When people are studying the Bible together, they shouldn't think that this ministry is "lesser" than "real" ministry, which happens elsewhere.

This mutual ministry isn't just teaching either. That is the most common ministry described in the New Testament, but it's not the only one. There's also encouraging, exhorting, comforting, rebuking, training, correcting, spurring on, and more. Much of that happens alongside teaching; as you teach, you may rebuke or exhort someone. But much of it happens in spontaneous and organic interactions; someone shares how they are doing, and you respond, and what you say encourages them. You pray for someone in a small-group setting, and your prayer spurs someone on to live for Jesus. That variety of ministries is harder to spot because it doesn't usually get put on a weekly schedule, where you could identify it; it just happens as a community interacts and its members live life together. And that is exactly the type of mutual interaction, with a variety of dynamics, that should make up ministry in churches shaped by the New Testament.

We need to embrace this multicoloured picture of ministry—both in who is involved and in what is happening—rather than being monochrome. That's what we see in the image of the church as a body in 1 Corinthians 12 and Romans 12. The picture of the body represents both unity—since we are one body—and difference—since we are different parts. And each part of the body has a part to play in the building of the whole:

> *There are different kinds of gifts, but the same Spirit distributes them. There are different kinds of service, but the same Lord. There are different kinds of working, but in all of them and in everyone it is the same God at work. Now to each one the manifestation of the Spirit is given for the common good. (1 Corinthians 12:4-7)*

Paul's point here is that people make different contributions, but it is all the same God working or the same Spirit gifting, and it is all for the good of the one body.

It's important and significant to see that there is no gender differentiation in these passages. Rather, they portray mutual ministry within church life where everyone contributes and everyone receives. Taking these passages seriously means we must expect men to be ministered to by women, including through teaching, encouraging, correcting, and so on. I (Graham) can testify to the helpful teaching and encouragement I've received from women in my small group, even as one of the elders.

At this point you might be asking, "But how does this fit with Paul's prohibition in 1 Timothy 2:12 of women teaching or exercising authority over men?" This is where the difference between "big-T Teaching" and "small-t teaching" comes into play. As we saw in chapter 5, there is a certain type of teaching that women are not to exercise over men in the church. This raises the question as to what aspects of church life count as "big-T Teaching" (small groups, seminars, and so on?), and we'll return to that in our final chapters. But in order for women *never* to teach men in *any* way, men and women would need to live on different planets! Women (small-t) teach men in a variety of ways every day, and this is good and right.

It's a little like a sports team. The coach sets the overall direction for the players and leads the training sessions. But players should still learn from each other and encourage each other. There is overall leadership and mutuality alongside each other.

EVERY PART MATTERS

One of Paul's main points in 1 Corinthians 12 is that everyone's contribution is needed and should be valued. He deals with the issue of perceived inferiority in verse 15:

> *Now if the foot should say, "Because I am not a hand, I do not belong to the body," it would not for that reason stop being part of the body. (1 Corinthians 12:15)*

Some people in the Corinthian church seemed to think that because they didn't have a certain gift, they weren't really part of the body. They felt like second-class citizens. Paul's response is to say that the whole point of the body is that it has many different parts; if they were all eyes, then the body wouldn't be able to hear (verses 16-17). Whether you're a "foot" or a "hand", your contribution to the life of the church is needed and necessary.

Paul also then deals with the issue of perceived superiority. It seems that some people felt that they didn't need the gifts of some others—they could manage on their own. So Paul says:

The eye cannot say to the hand, "I don't need you!"
And the head cannot say to the feet, "I don't need you!"
(1 Corinthians 12:21)

Paul says that God has put the body together, and he knew what he was doing. He has designed it to have this mutual inter-dependence for the good of all. So, we ought to welcome and value the contribution of all. If we think we could eliminate a group of people from church life, and think we would still grow just as well, we've got this wrong.

Our concern is that among complementarian churches, there can be a tendency to assume or give the impression that we don't really need the ministry of women—which is to relegate half of the body as being unnecessary. Paul says you can't think like that. In our embracing of complementarianism, there must not only be space for but also the encouragement of this variety of ministries, with everyone—including women—playing their part. Any reduction of what counts as ministry, or any narrowing of whose contribution is really needed, or any limiting of what types of ministries are of value, will have a knock-on effect. The ministries of women in church life must be not simply permitted but pursued if the body is to grow as it's supposed to.

COMMENDED AS CO-WORKERS

We can see the same idea in a brief survey of the contribution of women to ministry in Scripture.

There are many examples of churches that meet in women's homes: those of Mary (Acts 12:12), Lydia (16:40), Chloe (1 Corinthians 1:11), and Nympha (Colossians 4:15). We can add Priscilla and Aquila as a married couple who hosted a church, and note that Priscilla is named specifically (Romans 16:3-5; 1 Corinthians 16:19). In opening their homes, these women were acting as significant supporters and patrons of the church, and it is most likely that they acted as host in some way.

We also see women who are described as working or labouring in the gospel. For example:

> *Help these women since they have contended at my side*
> *in the cause of the gospel, along with Clement and the*
> *rest of my co-workers, whose names are in the book of life.*
> *(Philippians 4:3)*

> *Greet Tryphena and Tryphosa, those women who work hard*
> *in the Lord. Greet my dear friend Persis, another woman*
> *who has worked very hard in the Lord. (Romans 16:12)*

See the phrases Paul uses? "Contended at my side"; "co-workers"; "worked hard in the Lord". Those are the kinds of words used of people like Timothy and Titus. These are not second-class descriptions! In our churches have we turned the volume up on passages that limit the role of women and not heard these ringing commendations?

As I (Graham) have reflected on this, I've realised that my instinct is not always to value the contributions of women in this way. This came home to me when hearing a talk by the Bible teacher Jen Wilkin in which she asked whether we believe that the contribution of women is *essential* for the advance of the kingdom. And I realised that although I *kind of* did, I wouldn't have asserted it that clearly or firmly. For many people, both men and women, the assumption is that the contribution of women is nice but not necessary—helpful but not essential.

Church leaders, whatever roles you decide women may undertake in your church—whatever they do or don't do— how *you feel* about those roles, and how valuable you think they are, will show itself. Do you give the impression that women are essential co-workers? Or are they helpful extras? What we think here will be very significant in shaping the culture of our churches.

SIMILARITIES AND DIFFERENCES IN MINISTRY

This leads to the question: what differences should we expect to see between men and women doing ministry? In churches like the one in Philippi, Paul obviously worked with other people, including women whom he regarded as co-workers. But were there things that the women did that Paul didn't do? Or that Paul did that women didn't?

But maybe it's slightly the wrong question. Granted, we'd expect that overall leadership and authoritative teaching would be given by qualified male elders. But the question itself presumes difference and not similarity. There's a helpful parallel in the example of parenting. Picture a dad and a mum parenting their children: What does the dad do that the mum doesn't? Or the mum do that the dad doesn't? Surely, they both teach, encourage, care, comfort and discipline. While they might have different strengths and weaknesses, it's not that parenting means one thing for one of them that it doesn't for the other, or that parenting looks different between them. But they do parent in the context of a marriage where the husband lovingly leads and the wife respectfully submits. There's a shape to their marriage and so a shape to their parenting; but parenting itself isn't one thing for one person and something else for the other.

Does that provide an analogy for ministry? Ministry doesn't mean one thing for a man and another thing for a woman, but all ministry is done within the context of male leadership within the church. So, we expect women to teach, correct, rebuke and encourage, just as men should, and vice versa. While there are overall leadership roles given to men, there are no passages suggesting that the mutual ministry of the church looks different for men than for women.

I (Graham) once attended a day conference on evangelism which was aimed at pastors and evangelists. I took along a female staff member from my church, as she was a gifted evangelist. She was the only woman at the conference—and that was revealing in itself. But during the afternoon tea break, someone asked if she'd help in the kitchen with serving refreshments and clearing away. Why ask her? Presumably because they instinctively felt that the conference was less for her than for the men, or that she was better suited to that task than the men were. Whatever background and assumptions might shape these sorts of instincts, we need to identify and expose them. Otherwise, we will make unwarranted moves in restricting women's contributions in ministry.

Having underlined the similarities—ministry is not a different thing for men and for women—we should also remember the differences we've discussed between men and women in previous chapters. On average, men and women have different traits and perspectives, and those will flow out in how they do ministry. While ministry will still involve teaching, men and women will tend to teach in different ways, with different emphases and styles.

The author Jonathan Leeman writes about the similarity there will be in discipleship and service in the church (apart from the role of elder being limited to men); however, he then goes on:

> If God created us male and female, women possess a way of being human that men don't, which means they possess ways of disciple-making that men don't, however we might articulate those differences of being and doing.[46]

The ministry of a church will then be all the richer for those differences. Teaching will be enhanced in its perspectives, encouragement will be more rounded in its approach, and comfort will take on different shapes depending on who is giving it. All of which is for the good and the growth of the church.

The complementarity between the genders means it is to the detriment of the church if ministry by women is minimised or marginalised. So, rightly understood, complementarianism is an argument for how essential the contribution of women is.

REFLECTIONS

It can sometimes be that male church leaders feel they only need to deal with the issue of women's contributions to ministry if someone raises it. When someone does raise it, then the reaction can be, "Oh dear, we're going to have to deal with this". But what we've seen here means that church leaders should be thinking this through and looking to promote the ministry of women, in all the roles they believe are good and right. Otherwise, there is the danger of women not playing their part as they could and should, to the detriment of the health of the church.

The speaker and writer Jen Wilkin puts this well:

> *How sweet a thing when a woman of apparent ministry gifting elicits from male leadership not "Oh, no," but "At last!" God help complementarians if we spend our energies fastidiously chalking the boundaries of a racecourse we never urge or equip our women to run.*[47]

So how might women's perspectives and contributions come into play in the life of your church? We assume that there will be forms of ministry by women to women, such as we see described in Titus 2:4-5; our point here, though, is that such ministry is not the totality of their contributions. Exactly what women do and don't do will depend on what each church thinks is appropriate, and we'll discuss more on that in a later chapter. For now, here are some ideas of ways in which women might complement men.

EXAMPLES FROM GRAHAM

Small groups

I am in a mixed-gender small group in my church. I benefit enormously from the insight, perspective, encouragement, and prayers of both men and women. Single-sex small groups have certain advantages: they make some sensitive conversations easier, they can lead to more open sharing, and more. In some ways it is just *easier* to have single-sex groups. But it can also be *poorer*—because we lose the richness of complementarity between the sexes. We lose the contributions that those men or women would make to our discipleship. I'm not saying that there's no place for single-sex groups, but I would want to argue for the normality of mixed groups because we're to live out our discipleship together ministering to each other.

Input into eldership discussions

At my church we have a male eldership, and we're convinced that's right. But I've known the experience of the elders discussing something, deciding on a plan of action, and then going home and chatting with their wives. The next day an email is sent saying, "I was talking to my wife and wonder if we need to reconsider..." Lots of people I know in ministry have had that experience.

There are several possible explanations. It could be that the elders are being a bit passive and abdicating responsibility, bowing to whatever their wife thinks is best rather than stepping up and leading. It could be that discussion with anyone outside the group of elders would have brought a different perspective. But it could also be that some of the wives have a different perspective because they are women, and that should be welcomed and encouraged. In which case, I'd much prefer to seek input from women before we make decisions, so that we are fully informed when we have that discussion. I also don't want the contributions of women to be restricted to those who happen to be married to the elders (helpful as they are).

So, at our church we are exploring ways of have some sounding-board-type groups with a mix of people in them. For example, we currently run our elders' agenda past our staff team—which includes women—so that they can ask questions or make comments ahead of our discussion. That has made the elders more aware of issues or questions that we would not have otherwise considered, resulting in a much more rounded discussion as elders.

Input into preaching

One thing I have done with regard to preaching is to have a sermon "preview" group. I send out a draft of my sermon script to a variety of people, who read through it and feed back thoughts and comments. At various times there have been women in that group who have provided a perspective I had missed, either on the passage itself or on the way I was expressing things. I remain responsible for what I decide to say, but their perspectives have enriched and balanced the final sermons in really helpful ways.

Other pastors I know discuss the sermon passage with a mixed group of people (say, their staff team) earlier in the week. That gives them a chance to hear how the passage strikes people, what questions it raises, and what application areas emerge. This is helpful for a number of reasons, but not least because the input of women can often alert a male preacher to perspectives he wouldn't have thought of.

EXAMPLES FROM JANE

Women on staff ministry teams

I have had the privilege of serving on several ministry teams full-time both in the context of local church ministry and at a theological college. Each one of my bosses has been a committed complementarian, and working with each one has been a joy. These men have had women on staff, full-time and part-time, and have highly valued them—seeking to use their gifts, and to train and equip them further in a variety of ministries.

Slots and spots in church

At churches I have been part of in the past, we've had occasional slots as part of the service, in which someone shares for 5-7 minutes on an aspect connected to the sermon. These slots don't take the place of the preacher doing application, but are a further way in which the church family can see how God's word applies to us. These have included testimonies (about initial conversion and also about living as a Christian), book reviews, presentations on church history, doctrine and ministry skills, and interviews.

At my current church we have something called "Everyday discipleship spots" where, ahead of time, my pastor asks someone—often the person who is leading in prayer—to share something they have recently learnt, been convicted about or encouraged by, and so on. Some of the things people have shared are, for example: how we learn from other Christians, personal Bible-reading and prayer patterns, being a father, suffering, honouring parents as an adult child, and what they have learnt recently in their Christian book club.

The advantages of these kinds of slots and spots include: more people's gifts from the congregation are used and recognised, and this can then lead to them being involved in other ministries; they help the congregation to get to know each other better, and the staff to get to know their congregation; they encourage church members to pastorally care for each other, and to talk about Christian things after the formal church meeting has ended; they help people to not be passive consumers but to exercise more ownership of church.

All these things are true whether the person upfront doing the spot is male or female. Yet as we have mentioned earlier, a woman can bring something to it that a man cannot, and vice versa, just by virtue of their sex.

The ideas I have mentioned may sound really obvious. Yet often they just don't happen—even in churches that have no theological problem with them. One reason why they don't happen is simply that in the busyness of church life they are not planned. These spots happen more easily when a staff member takes the initiative, but a church member could take the initiative and ask a staff member/elder about them—it just may be that the staff member/elder has never thought of the idea before or that it has fallen off their radar.

When trying these kinds of things out, we won't always know how well they will work or the benefits they bring until after they have been done! Often we're reluctant to give new things a try just in case they don't work out. But if you believe this is consistent with your understanding of complementarianism, it really is worth trying them out. Much will depend on who is doing it, the length of time they speak for, and how experienced they are at public speaking. There may be times when we need to have difficult conversations afterwards to assess the contribution—but if we don't try, we'll only ever stick to current patterns of ministry.

Women co-ordinating prayer time in a mixed-sex Bible-study group

An older married couple who are dear friends of mine have been co-leading a Bible-study group for decades.

Complementarians have different views on women teaching in a mixed Bible-study setting. My friends have decided that the husband will lead the Bible study, and his wife will co-ordinate the prayer time. She has extraordinary gifts in pastoral care. She is relationally very in tune and an excellent listener. She remembers group members' points from the previous weeks. But she also doesn't avoid asking difficult questions! Along with drawing prayer points from the study and asking group members to share requests, sometimes she will choose an additional focus, such as one of the missionaries linked with their church or an aspect of concern in general society.

For some readers, how my friends have worked out their Bible study co-leading is too conservative. For others it is not conservative enough. But it's a great example of how a husband and wife can work together, with love and respect for and joy in each other. They've found a way of partnering that goes "with the grain" of their individual gifting, what they think is right from God's word, and what they feel comfortable with.

HOW WILL YOUR CHURCH GROW?

How will your church grow? It will grow "as each part does its work" (Ephesians 4:16). We've seen how essential it is to have a multi-coloured variety of ministries by men and women in order for that growth to happen. That will require specific decisions about what men and women do and don't do in church life—decisions we've referred to but haven't yet tackled. That's where we're going next.

REFLECTION QUESTIONS
For individuals
1. What do you instinctively think of as the key ministry in your church?
2. Do you have an appropriate appreciation of the breadth and variety of ministries needed for growth?
3. What did you find challenging and/or encouraging about the examples of women ministering in the New Testament?
4. Where have you witnessed the interplay of similarities and differences in the way that men and women do ministry?
5. What did you make of the examples Graham and Jane gave? Can you think of others?

For a group
1. What is considered a "key" ministry in your church? How do you think church members would answer that question?
2. Do you think your church has an appropriate appreciation of the breadth and variety of ministries needed for growth?
3. What is challenging and/or encouraging about the examples of women ministering in the New Testament?
4. Do you think you rightly hold in view both the similarities and differences in ministry between men and women?
5. How might the examples Graham and Jane gave fit within your church? What else might work well?

8.
Coming in to Land

"**S**o, what do we actually do?!"

That's the key question that gets asked about complementarianism: what is it meant to look like in practice? What roles should men and women play in church life? This is where the rubber hits the road. We've anticipated, but held off from, this question so far because we've wanted to go broader and deeper first. That has hopefully spared us from the dangers we identified in the opening chapter. If we jump to application too quickly, we easily end up with superficial answers.

But we do need to answer this question. We're going to do that in two stages. First, this chapter looks at key decisions that church leaders need to make, and then, in the next chapter, we'll look at how to go about implementing those decisions in the nitty-gritty of church life.

IDENTIFY BIBLICAL CONVICTIONS

We face two common temptations when organising church life. The first is traditionalism, where we do whatever we've always done. The second is pragmatism, where we do whatever we think works best. Both are common issues when working out complementarianism.

Traditionalism means that we always run with the decisions of the past, and our practice is never really questioned or re-examined. The label "traditionalism" can make it sound as if those practices must be very old, but that's not always the case: the principle is only that you perpetuate what's been done before (except maybe with minor modifications around the edges). Previous practice always wins, whether it's 10 years or 100 years old. We should, of course, have great respect for tradition, and there's no need to change things unnecessarily, but traditionalism goes beyond that. At its worst, traditionalism excuses us from ever developing convictions of our own. It's a way of outsourcing decisions that we should make to those in the past.

Pragmatism is doing whatever we think will work or seems to be working elsewhere. It means we'll be very happy to change our practice in the hope of achieving more or doing things better. It often goes hand in hand with functional views of church. Church is seen primarily as a place for teaching, evangelism, discipleship and so on—so whatever seems to maximise these is what the pragmatist will choose.

We should not be anti-pragmatic and should recognise that there are better and worse ways of doing things—but fundamentally, we should want to operate out of convictions first. At its worst, pragmatism is all about gaining results. It's a church version of "the end justifies the means".

We've mentioned a key word in contrast to traditionalism or pragmatism, and that is "convictions". Each of us should want to have biblical convictions about church life and ministry. In this chapter we'll talk through some key areas, but a word of explanation first: we're not expecting every reader to agree with our convictions or how they then get worked out in church life. In fact, we don't agree precisely on that outworking between ourselves! While we'll happily try to convince you of what we do think, our greater concern is to help you have your own convictions and live them out yourself.

CONVICTIONS ABOUT COMPLEMENTARIAN MINISTRY

Broad theological convictions

One of my (Jane's) colleagues suggests six principles of complementarian ministry. As you can see from the list below, these principles would apply equally well to any topic about which we had questions from Scripture.[48] Maybe this surprises you—or maybe you feel disappointed, as perhaps you were expecting something you had never heard before! But ultimately, the simplicity of this list is great news for us. It shows us how accessible understanding complementarianism is. And it reminds us that if we are to truly get what God is saying to us about the ministries of men and women, we need to begin with—and keep coming back to—God's unfolding plan of salvation and what it has to say about men and women. If we don't do this, we will have a "complementarianism" that really doesn't have much to do with Christ and his plans for his church. It is all too easy, in discussions about the ministries of men and women, to be so distracted about things such as rights, equality and gifting that the focus ends up being on us rather than on our Lord Jesus Christ. These six principles help serve as an antidote to that problem, as they keep us anchored in the main concern of God's word.

- We need to think and act in light of *eternity*
    - We cannot take our cue from the world.
    - Rather, we need to hear the gospel and live the gospel of eternal salvation.

- God's *creation* is very good, so our gendered relationships are a good gift from God.
    - The Bible: Genesis 1:27, 2:18; 1 Corinthians 11:8-12; 1 Timothy 2:13
    - When it comes to relationships between men and

women, both equality and order are true and must
be affirmed.

- Human *sin* is serious and devastating, especially when it
comes to relationships between men and women.
    - The Bible: Genesis 3:12-17; 1 Timothy 2:14
    - We have a real problem on our hands, and we can't
    be naïve.

- *Christ's redeeming work* really makes a difference to the way
we relate to one another as men and women.
    - The Bible: Galatians 3:28; 1 Corinthians 11:3;
    Ephesians 5:1-2, 22-31; Colossians 3:12-19; 1 Peter
    2:13-3:7; 1 Timothy 2:5-6, 8-15
    - Christ brings life and order.
    - Christ brings service, love and respect.
    - We seek to redeem complementarity, not obliterate it.

- The world needs more than anything to hear *the gospel*
through men and women working together.
    - The Bible:
        * Women involved in ministry in the New
        Testament: Mary Magdalene, Joanna, Mary the
        mother of James, Lydia, Priscilla with Aquila,
        Phoebe, Mary, Junia with Andronicus, Tryphena
        and Tryphosa, Persis, Rufus' mother.
        * Word ministries of women: 1 Corinthians
        11:2-16; Titus 2:3-4; 1 Timothy 3:11
        * Complementary roles of men and women:
        1 Corinthians 11:2-16; 14:26-35; 1 Timothy
        2:8-15
    - This is a gospel agenda, not a feminist agenda.
    - This is a gospel agenda, not a "women's issue".

- As God's fellow-workers, we must keep *struggling* through
the Spirit against our sin and weakness in our efforts to

work together for the gospel as men and women.
  - The Spirit is at work, yet we are still in the flesh.
  - Our flesh will default to Genesis 3.
  - We need to struggle against many sins—and to
    forgive.

These principles provide the broad structure for all our
thinking about complementarianism. Many of the points
mentioned have been discussed in previous chapters. But
now we need to drill into some more specifics. In particular,
church leaders must establish their convictions from Scripture
on three key areas: 1) teaching and authority; 2) whole-church
life; and 3) men and women in general.

Convictions about teaching and authority

The first area in which we need convictions is on the nature
of teaching and authority in the life of the church. We saw in
chapter 5 that the passages limiting the role of women revolve
around these areas. So the question which we must have an
answer for is this: what exactly does Scripture prohibit women
from doing?

In chapter 5 we considered 1 Timothy 2:12, where Paul
says, "I do not permit a woman to teach or to assume
authority over a man". A key issue in this verse is how the
teaching and the authority relate to each other. Some people
take them separately and so say that women should neither
teach men nor have any authority over a man. Taken fully,
that would lead to no woman ever being in a position of
authority, such as leading a team within church life. And that
would be so even if the task had nothing to do with teaching
(such as, say, a refreshments team). Nor would a woman ever
be permitted to teach a man in any context.

Others understand the teaching and authority as
distinguishable but connected. They are ideas that go hand

in hand and "bleed" into each other. Understood that way, the verse is not saying that women shouldn't teach at all, but that they should not teach in a way that exercises a particular "elder-type" authority over a man. Likewise, it's not that a woman can't have any authority over a man, but that they should not have authority in a way connected to teaching them. This usually means that limitations on what women can do revolve around leadership positions and key teaching roles.

Others take the teaching and authority as one concept: authoritative teaching in the life of the church. This often translates into fewer restrictions on what women can do— women are only restricted from authoritative pronouncements on doctrine in the church, but can teach, preach and lead in most other ways.

We (Graham and Jane) basically sit in the second category ourselves and commented on this back in chapter 5. We hope you can see how significant this is: being clear on what your convictions are with regards to teaching and authority shapes all that follows.

Convictions about whole-church life

We mustn't just have convictions about any limitations on the role of women. We must also have convictions about what church life looks like. This goes back to our chapters on church and ministry. What are your convictions about the "one another" commands, including women ministering to men? What are your convictions about the church as a body, where everyone plays a part? What are your resulting convictions about everyone benefitting from other people's ministries, including men benefitting from women? What are your resulting convictions about the necessity of women's contribution for the good of the church (rather than just its niceness)?

This is where we must put the "limitation" passages and the "whole-body" passages together. Remember how Paul regarded women as co-workers who laboured with him. What are your convictions on this?

Convictions about men and women

Lastly, what convictions do you have about men and women in general (as opposed to their roles)? About their equality and complementarity? Their value and dignity? Their significance in church life and discipleship? This goes back to our earlier chapters exploring gender. These convictions show themselves less clearly in specific roles or positions in church, but they do show themselves. They are more like the foundation we are building on, or the air we are breathing, while we go about everything else. They will contribute to what it "feels" like being a man or a woman, regardless of what you can or can't do.

I (Graham) once had the disturbing experience of speaking to a female church member who said that church life felt "claustrophobic" for women. It was disturbing because I wanted nothing of the kind—I wanted women to flourish. But somehow, that wasn't coming across—and it was less to do with what women were doing and more to do with this "feel".

MAPPING ONTO CHURCH LIFE

Having established convictions about these areas, we then need to map them onto to church life. This is where being as clear as we can be on our conviction is crucial. We can easily say we are complementarian but then stick with traditionalism or run with pragmatism. Instead, we want to follow through on our convictions. There are a few key areas to work through here.

Church polity / leadership

Every church has some way of being led, organising itself and making decisions. This is usually called your church "polity".

For instance, classically Anglican churches have a vicar (and sometimes an assistant called a curate), a church council, church wardens and sometimes trustees. Baptist churches will often have a pastor, maybe an assistant pastor, and then a diaconate. Many independent churches have a pastor and an eldership, and a diaconate. Presbyterian churches are often similar. Others use different terminology for the groups involved, such as a "leadership team".

Our concern here is not to argue which of these polities is biblical or best (there are other books on that) but to point out that you need to map your complementarian convictions onto whatever your structure is. That means thinking through the roles and responsibilities of the different positions and groups and how they connect to the teaching and authority we've been discussing. In an Anglican church, for example, you'd need to decide what a church warden was responsible for before deciding if it's a role open to men and women.

Many churches draw a line around the group called "elders". As we saw in chapter 5, this group is responsible for the overall teaching and life of the church, and so complementarian churches commonly limit this role to men. With other roles, such as deacons or leadership committees, it will vary, depending on what those people are responsible for. You need to decide how "elder-like" some roles are; or how much they are concerned with the "teaching/authority" in the life of the church.

Staff team / volunteers

We need a similar exercise with a church staff team or key volunteer positions. For the purposes of this exercise, what makes a position "key" is not whether someone is employed to do it, but the function that role plays within the life of the church. This connects with the polity question because some of these roles are the same. For example, an employed pastor is usually one of the elders, alongside lay elders who volunteer their time. But there may be additional positions on a church staff team, such as an evangelist, a women's worker, a pastoral care worker or a counsellor, and so on. There are also often key roles such as small-group leaders or youth-group leaders. Again, we need to ask what these roles involve and so how our convictions map on to them.

If your overall conviction is that the role of elder is limited to men, a key question to ask is this: To what extent is this role (of, say, a Bible-study leader or an evangelist) that of an elder? Or is it a role conducted under the oversight of the elders?

Other roles and functions

Lastly, we need to consider other roles and functions in church life. This is where it can get tricky, as we try to map our convictions onto the various ways in which our church works and the variety of things it does. Consider the variety of roles and functions in your church. For instance, you probably have corporate church services with prayers, readings, singing, the Lord's Supper, baptism, preaching and more. Different people take part in these services in different ways. Who should do what? In addition, your church probably has some sort of small-group structure for study, prayer, support and fellowship. Who should lead these groups overall, or lead studies or prayer times within them? We could keep going with other areas such as evangelism, social-care/mercy-ministry projects, training courses, and more.

Within all these various aspects of church life, who should do what? Once again, the key question is what teaching and authority is or are being expressed in any setting. Or, to what extent is this is an eldership role? Those are really two ways into the same territory.

Take, for example, the question of preaching. Our conviction is that regular preaching in the life of the church is an eldership role, because it is giving authoritative teaching and exercising leadership over the whole congregation. We recognise that some differ from us in this. For example, as we saw in chapter 5, some suggest that preaching that happens in churches today is an example of the type of "small-t teaching" that both male and female believers are called to, according to gifting (Romans 12:7-8), rather than the type of authoritative, "big-T teaching" that is prohibited in 1 Timothy 2:12.[49] As such, non-elders, including women, can preach, as long as it is under the authority of the elders. For others, it's a matter of frequency: if someone preaches frequently, they take on the de facto role of an elder, but occasional sermons by women are fine. In contrast, we would argue that the exercise of authority is inherent in the act of preaching and so the two cannot be separated out. However, we do recognise that it depends both on the precise convictions of the church regarding teaching and authority (as outlined above) and also on how preaching itself is understood.

This also raises the question of whether anyone who isn't an elder can preach—regardless of whether they are a man or a woman. Many churches allow men who aren't elders to preach, in which case, we need to ask what dynamic is in play there and why women cannot do the same. Some will prohibit women (but not all non-elders) from preaching purely on the basis of the restriction in 1 Timothy 2, which they regard as separate to the question of eldership. Others will say that the person preaching is being invited by the elders to speak and does so on their behalf; and that the limitation to men is appropriate because of having a male eldership—since the eldership is male, their "spokesperson" is to be male too.

As we saw in chapter 6, there are lots of other ways people can contribute to a corporate service, including within the teaching. For example, at Graham's church there is often a "contributions and questions" time following the sermon (or within it), and women and men make great comments that add to and enrich what the preacher has said. We have also had men and women reflect on the passage and the sermon ahead of time and then give a reflection following the sermon as to what had struck them or how they thought it applied. You might have a woman contribute on a specific topic along with teaching from an elder. But exactly what you do will depend on how you have pinned down your convictions.

This process of mapping convictions onto roles and functions will not always be clear-cut; much depends on the different dynamics in play. This can be difficult because we can tend to prefer black-and-white decisions where we know whether something is right or wrong! But sometimes things aren't so straightforward—they require wisdom. A further complication is that the dynamics are not constant but can change.

The types of dynamics we need to consider include:

- *Relational aspects*
  Who is it that is doing it? What is their Christian maturity? Are they older or younger, male or female? What power do they have within the church and within the broader society? We see the necessity of taking into consideration relational dynamics in 1 Timothy 5:1-2. Two different people can do the same ministry, but they can each come across quite differently.

- *Regularity and timing*
  The more regular a ministry is in church, and the greater time it takes up in a church service or other context, the greater weight it tends to have, and so the more authority it conveys to congregation members. This will vary depending greatly on who is doing it (so it connects to relational dynamic above) and also the content of what is happening (see the chart below).

- *Personal or public nature of the ministry*

	Personal / Private	Public
Mutual encouragement / exhortation	E.g. speaking with one another after church; one to one meeting	E.g. singing; sharing a testimony; ministry-skills training session
Elders / shepherd	E.g. church discipline	E.g. regular Sunday sermon

The chart above is a simple tool that helps us see that generally speaking (no pun intended!), there are two types of word ministries—personal and public. The level of authority being exercised, though, lies in a combination of whether the setting is public or personal and the content of the ministry itself. Hence in private an elder might give an authoritative warning over a matter of church discipline (before it might become public). In a one-to-one meeting between church members, there may also be warnings given, but they shouldn't have the same authority invested in them.

In public there is generally greater authority being exercised, but that again depends on the nature of what is happening. Sharing a testimony exercises far less guidance to a congregation than preaching a sermon. And even in studying Scripture, there's a difference between helping each other understand the text, and the deciding of what that means for us as a church.

Complementarians will inevitably vary in how their convictions play out in practice. For instance, some will feel a women can lead parts of a public service, while others will not. In fact we (Graham and Jane) have slightly different opinions on that issue. Our point for now is for the need to think and reflect, rather than falling back on traditionalism or pragmatism.

A FULL MAPPING EXERCISE

We need to be aware that it's possible to go through this mapping exercise and only end up with what women cannot do. For example, saying that they cannot be elders, and that they cannot preach in a corporate church context. While we believe that these conclusions are good and right, that's not the whole story. For this to be a full mapping exercise, we must decide what women can be doing and how they will contribute to all areas of church life. And it will mean encouraging that in practice. If women can teach in certain contexts such as small groups, if they can contribute in public services, if they can play a key part in evangelism, and if their contribution to mutual ministries in the church is needed, then we need to say so and do so. We'll say more on this in the next chapter.

But women can also contribute in various ways beyond existing roles and functions. For example, we mentioned in a previous chapter the idea of women giving a perspective within decisions in church life that might complement those of the (male) elders. Assuming a decision is the responsibility of the elders, they cannot and should not farm out that decision to others. But it is good and right that they get input and ideas from others. And if you think (as we do) that both men and women will contribute importantly in this process, then it's incumbent on the elders to make sure that happens.

SO WHAT SHOULD WE DO?

So what should we do? Hopefully you're a long way further forward in answering that question. Establish your convictions first and foremost; don't rush to make a decision on particular practices. And beware of having your convictions shaped only by making decisions about practice—that's the wrong way round.

Then move to map your convictions onto the variety of ministries in church life—structures, positions, roles and so on. Some areas may appear clear and straightforward; others may feel confused and messy. Remember, we could fail to obey God in two ways here. We could ignore what he says about the right leadership of men; or ignore what he says about the necessary ministry of women. Try to focus on the dynamics in play rather than on what's always been done or what seems most pragmatic. And be prepared to say, "We're not sure what's right here. Let's discuss and pray together." Our gracious God "gives generously" to those who ask for wisdom (James 1:5).

In our last chapter we'll think about the practicalities of leading this sort of process and change in a local church setting.

REFLECTION QUESTIONS
For individuals
1. Why do the "broad theological convictions" listed on pages 115-116 matter so much?
2. What convictions do you have in each of the three areas listed on pages 117-119?
3. How do you feel about how this maps onto to church life?
4. Where are the debated areas of application for you?

For a group
1. Why do the "broad theological convictions" listed on page 115-116 matter so much?
2. Where does our church land on the other theological convictions listed on pages 117-119?
3. Have we done this kind of mapping exercise?
4. Are there areas of inconsistency in our practice?
5. What areas of application are most contested or debated in our church? Why?

9.

Putting It into Practice

I (Jane) regularly get asked by men and women: "Do you think that a woman doing this [insert particular thing] at church/Bible study is ok?" Perhaps, by this point in the book, you're looking for an answer to that kind of question. We're reluctant to give you a list of "Do's and Don'ts" because so much depends on what your precise convictions are, along with your context and culture. But we do want to get practical.

The focus of this book is on embracing complementarianism in our churches and, as with any other biblical truth, we are only embracing complementarianism if we are living it out, since true knowledge is relational. So, in this chapter we'll talk through how we might approach implementation in a local church.

LEADERS FIRST

First, the leaders of a church need to take responsibility and decide where they will land on this issue. As we mentioned in the previous chapter, different churches will have different leadership structures. For the sake of simplicity, we will refer to church leaders as the elders, as that is the common biblical word. Elders should lead on this issue because, as we saw in chapter 5, they have the ultimate responsibility for shepherding the flock by teaching them what is right from

God's word and guarding them against false teaching. So, elders need to first work out their convictions and map that onto church life, as we saw in the previous chapter.

But then the elders need to *lead the church into* the convictions and pattern of ministry they have landed on. That is not an easy task! It involves:

1. being clear on their convictions and application of complementarianism.
2. considering the context and wider culture of their church.
3. communicating this vision with others.
4. implementing this in practice.

Those are the steps we'll work through. In the last chapter we talked through areas of conviction that need to be clarified and then the exercise of mapping those onto church life. This chapter fills that out and gives some suggestions of how to go about it for your church.

BEING CLEAR ON CONVICTIONS AND APPLICATION

Clarity is key. Even being clear on what you are and aren't clear on is helpful! In other words, be willing to say where you have decided convictions and where you still have questions. How you establish this clarity will depend on the polity of the church, but it will involve the elders studying, discussing and deciding together.

One option is for the elders to write a position paper which can be agreed on among themselves and later shared with others. Even if you decide not to write a substantial position paper, being able to articulate your convictions clearly will usually require writing something down, even if it is only a summary.

In trying to answer, "What do I think about complementarianism?" a friend of mine (Jane's) who is the senior pastor of a church wrote such a position paper. He said that it was difficult, taking him a lot of time and effort to work through the key passages, but that it was definitely worth it. It provided him with clarity as to what God's word was saying; that, in turn, led to a greater conviction and joy about complementarianism—and so he embraced complementarianism even more wholeheartedly than he had done previously. We must not lose sight of the fact that God's design for men and women is beautiful and beneficial for us.

A position paper will usually cover the same ground as the convictions and mapping exercise that we spoke about in the last chapter. It should include an articulation of the key principles you want to implement in church life and how you aim to work that out in practice. When it comes to implementing complementarian convictions in any one church, however, we also need to consider context and culture.

CONSIDERING CONTEXT AND CULTURE

None of us start from a blank slate. Your church will have certain practices and ways of working already in play. Along with those practices there will be a certain culture: who does what, how it is done and how it feels. In the mapping exercise, and particularly when starting to implement our decisions, we need to have a careful eye to this context and culture. We may be changing things in a way that people welcome—or equally, find unsettling. We risk miscommunicating if we don't give careful thought to how things might be interpreted or what feel they will give.

Answering questions such as the ones below may prove helpful for you in considering your church context and culture.

Leadership:
• What is the role and purpose of Christ's church?

- What is the role and purpose of an elder in a church?
- How do leaders here work together?
- How are leaders regarded by the membership?
- How have decisions been taken in the past?
- How does our leadership involve both men and women?

Church life and ministry:
- What ministries are currently happening in our church?
- What ministries have happened in the past at our church but are no longer happening? Why?
- What ministries do men and women do separately in our church?
- What ministries do men and women do together in our church?
- Does the church tend to run on the basis of traditionalism or pragmatism?
- How are different roles and functions regarded here?

Implementation:
- What do staff members and key lay leaders think about complementarianism?
- What range of opinion is there in the congregation about complementarianism?
- What difficulties and joys do I anticipate in speaking about this topic?
- What pushback do I think I'll get?

We should also consider the wider culture that our church is placed in:
- How are men and women regarded in this society?
- What roles do they tend to have in work and family?
- How would a complementarian position be regarded by those in our local community?

In considering these last questions we are not seeking to imitate or bow to the surrounding culture—rather, we look to live well and wisely in it. There will always be a difference between the church and the world such that we do not expect to fit in. However, there will also be an appropriate adaptation to a culture so as not to be unnecessarily different where we aren't required to be.

COMMUNICATION

Having decided what their convictions and applications look like, the leaders of a church need to communicate this to others. This is where holding and expressing clear convictions will be really key. We want to avoid simply telling people, "This is our position" or "We are doing it this way", without showing them that this is what God's word is actually saying. Elders are not to run churches where they just tell people what to believe! They should be giving their flock the tools to read the Bible for themselves, and enable them to weigh whether what the elders are saying is from Scripture. If a congregation member—male or female—does not think that what an elder is teaching is from the Bible, then there should be a clearly communicated way that they can bring this to the elder's or elders' attention without fear of repercussions.

Leading a church is a fundamentally relational exercise, and especially so over any highly charged issue. The leaders need to share their views with clarity, conviction and compassion. They are to be clear rather than fudge issues or avoid difficult areas. They are to be convinced in their own minds rather than apologetic, believing that God's word on this is both right and good for his people (although leaders should also be ready to revisit things, as we'll see). And they are to be compassionate towards those they lead, knowing that some may struggle with this teaching or have had bad experiences in the past, or that it will raise fears for them. For example, one couple that I (Graham) was speaking to pushed back against a complementarian position, but over time it appeared that one of their main concerns was for their unconverted grown-up children—they were worried that a complementarian position would put these children off the church even more. We need to speak gently in such situations, not shout louder.

We also want to communicate humbly. That means presenting views with confidence but listening to feedback and questions with respect. In most churches, presenting on complementarianism will result in much feedback! When I (Graham) most recently preached on this (because we were teaching through 1 Timothy and got to chapter 2), it raised many questions, which rumbled on for some time. That meant spending time listening carefully to people, not simply dismissing them as those who weren't prepared to hear what God was saying. (That moment may come, of course, but the first response is to listen.) This is particularly the case given the sensitivity over gender in our culture. If people's first response is to think that complementarianism is no different to oppression, then, while we must not capitulate, we must be compassionate and careful.

Sometimes people's questions may raise unanticipated issues. Being humble may mean needing to swallow your pride (and face up to your insecurities) and at times simply say, "I'm sorry, I need more time to figure this out before I give you an answer. I will go away and work on it and come back to you." Of course, in these instances, you need to go and work the issue out and then come back and communicate well, rather than just avoid the issue and hope it disappears!

INVOLVING OTHERS

If a paper has been written, then the elders might start by sharing this with any key leaders who were not involved in that process; that might be other staff members who aren't elders or other committees (for example, deacons or church councils), depending on the structure of your church. Care should be taken to involve a number of women. This process might result in you, as elders, revisiting issues, refining your position, and clarifying details before it is shared with the church more generally. This progression is good for a number of reasons:

- Elders may have missed key things that key leaders notice, and so the paper can be edited.
- It is good for the elders to hear what the key leaders all believe, and good for all the key leaders to hear what each other believes.
- It aids unity on this topic for the sake of the church.

In particular, elders should liaise with those involved in particular ministries, such as youth and children's workers, women's workers/pastors and small-group leaders. These groups will often have particular questions that relate to their area of ministry. Care should be taken to draw them into the conversation and make space to hear their input and their questions.

With regards to children's and youth ministry, we need to recognise that complementarianism is not just an issue for adults. Since we are born either male or female, it impacts even the youngest members of our church family. So it is key that those responsible for children's and youth ministry are clear on what God says about men and women, and how this impacts children and youth. It may be that you as elders decide to write a more detailed paper specific to those areas of ministry in conjunction with these leaders.

With regards to women's ministry, elders need to recognise the particular impact that their refined position will have on this area, both in what is done and in how it feels. It is crucial that elders engage appropriately here. Unfortunately, it has been the practice in some churches that the elders ask a woman to write a paper on complementarianism, rather than do so themselves, as if complementarianism is primarily a women's-ministry issue. (It's not, hence the name is not "women's ministry" but "complementarianism".) Or because they think women will know more about the issue. It can, of course, be the case that some women are clearer on this issue than many of their elders, as they've had reason to think it through. But elders must not abdicate their role here; rather, they should take the lead, in discussion with and while listening to those ministering specifically to women.

Small-group leaders may have specific questions about what is appropriate for that area of church life—for example, whether a woman can lead a small-group Bible study. This will again depend on the context and culture of your church, and whether or not you are proposing a change to the current status quo. Something that is a complete non-issue in some churches would represent a significant change in others!

This process of communication and involvement might happen in one "wave" or might take several "rounds", depending on the size and set-up of your church. However, in virtually any church setting, it is wise to get input from outside the eldership before finalising your position. People outside the eldership will bring a different perspective on the subject and an awareness of the congregation which will usually raise many issues worthy of consideration. That wider consultation must involve women—and listening carefully to their response. Once the elders have heard from such groups, they should be more aware of how the whole flock will receive and react to the position being proposed. This will ultimately help the whole church.

THE ART OF CONVERSATION

When speaking with these different people, elders should do all they can to promote the art of conversation.

- *Recognising, and expecting, that some may have a different view.*

- *Recognising that some may find it difficult to speak about this subject for a whole range of reasons.* These could include negative experiences with previous ministers, churches, or family situations. It may include the feeling from some that they are losing out on doing what they want to do but that the elders don't lose out on anything that they want to do. Or it could include theological differences such as someone's understanding of spiritual gifts.

- *Listening well.* The elders need to be prepared to learn from people and be interested in what they have to say. Church members need to know that the elders will weigh what they say against Scripture, while also being mindful of their church's context; and that they are open to being wrong. But elders also need to listen well to their members, as what they say is diagnostic about their life situation and also their beliefs. It is imperative that elders know what their members actually think; otherwise they can't truly pastor them.

- *Fostering a godly dynamic.* In your endeavour to listen well, elders should recognise that they have a lot of power and seek to use this to foster a dynamic whereby people can say what they actually believe without fear of being shut down—even if emotions get heightened. Each elder needs to make clear that there are open channels for dialogue, and this is more likely to happen if they don't get defensive.

- *Being aware of posture.* An elder already has more authority than the members he is speaking with, by virtue of being an elder. He may also be older than them, and be more well thought-out and so more articulate about these matters—after all, he has just written a paper on it together with others! He is also likely to be highly proficient in the usual language of the church, whereas some congregation members may not have this as their first or even second language. He is also likely to be physically taller and stronger, and have a deeper voice than most of the women (and some men), and so he potentially could come across as intimidating if things get more heated. None of these "advantages" should be used to manipulate a conversation.

Here's an example of what this might look like. One woman I (Jane) know was looking for a new church, and she wanted to find one where women preached Sunday sermons. She emailed a number of local churches, and all but one replied and told her their position on complementarianism. The exception was a pastor who instead replied with "Let's meet up for coffee". In their meeting she said what she believed, and he listened to her. He then said what he believed. She told me that she found the conversation so helpful and felt so listened to by this pastor that she decided to join his church, even though they did not have women preach sermons. Women preaching had been a very big issue for this woman. But by exercising the art of conversation, this elder released the pressure valve on the issue, and it changed her perspective on what she wanted in a church.

The vehicle through which you communicate with the wider church will depend on your church size and culture. There might be some upfront teaching on a Sunday; there might be a members' meeting in which to present and discuss. You might ask for feedback via small groups, as well as asking people to send in questions or speak to one of the leaders. It may be good to plan to have a couple of members' meetings over a certain period of time: for example, two or three meetings in six months. This has the benefit of maximising the number of congregation members who can attend, and helps members grow in their understanding and sense of ownership of complementarianism, as the whole church family has the opportunity to talk about a potentially difficult issue.

We find that some churches want to "out-source" teaching on some of the more controversial aspects of this subject to visiting speakers. But teaching on complementarianism primarily needs to come from the elders of the church. That is not to say that others—such as female staff or key women from the congregation—give no input upfront. Having men and women working together may indeed model exactly what you are teaching! There is a time and place for outside speakers too, but this tends to work best when the elders themselves have taught on complementarianism recently. If your church has a day or evening on the topic with a visiting speaker, the elders should be very much involved. It can be an emotional time for people. Elders know their congregation whereas outsiders generally do not. Additionally, if an elder always out-sources this topic, they potentially communicate to their flock that this area is extremely difficult to understand, and the normalcy of the issue is not necessarily conveyed.

In this vein, we want to underline that while writing a position paper is helpful for a number of reasons, the most important way that elders communicate to their congregations about complementarianism is through regular, expository, systematic teaching of the Bible. In this way the congregation can see where these passages are in the context of Scripture, and that it's not just a "hot topic" but part of the normal diet of Christian teaching and life. Remember that there are many passages in Scripture that teach us about complementarianism besides the central "obvious" ones.

PURSUING IN PRACTICE

It is not enough for elders to decide on their convictions, map that onto church life, discuss with key people and communicate well with the church. They then need to pursue this vision of complementarian ministry in practice.

For example, if elders have decided that it is good and right for women to contribute in services—say, in reading, praying, giving testimonies or reflections, or in leading a whole service—then they need to appropriately implement that. An unfortunately common scenario is that the elders land on a position and then ask a couple of women to do something, but they decline, and nothing ever changes. There may, of course, be lots of reasons why a woman is reluctant to speak up front, but the elders should be asking why. Is it that she isn't convinced that it is right to do? Is it that she doesn't think that it is her gift? Is it that training is needed? It is lack of confidence? Addressing these barriers is what we mean by pursuing in practice. It's not enough to just decide what you are happy to permit; you must pursue what you think is good!

In doing this there is a great need for open channels of communication and a willingness to listen: to ask how women feel about taking on new roles, or what kind of training or support would be helpful. And in doing this, men need to remember that their default assumptions about how to go about this may or may not work well for women! For example, in my (Graham's) church, a review of this area led us to want to have more women contributing in appropriate ways from the front as part of services. The elders decided how we would go about this and what training we would give. So we approached some women and worked with them in this area. It was well intentioned and had some reasonable results. However, the question was later raised: might it not have been good to have discussed with some key women how to best go about this process? Of course, the answer was "yes", and later we tried again, this time with more consultation and discussion.

We also think that, when it comes to making changes in practice, it's a good idea for elders to be willing to experiment and give things a try (unless, of course, you have decided that it is against your convictions). After trying something, it might be that the elders think, "Yes, it was good", or they might weigh it and decide, "Actually, no, we don't think that's an idea we'll repeat". But it is good to have some freedom—as long as things are evaluated afterwards—rather than being so worried about trying anything new that we are paralysed into doing nothing.

In pursuing our vision for complementarian ministry in our churches, we must work hard at this implementation in practice, but we must also continually hold up the vision we have. This is where we need to be aware of the subtle messaging that happens all the time in church life. For example, what are women commended for? If it's primarily for baking and child-care, then we are communicating something about their role and value. What are men commended for by contrast? Or, to change the question, what happens if a man volunteers to help look after kids in the creche? Is he applauded in a special way? What stereotypes might be used, say, in sermons? If talking about a particular job or profession, do we default to saying "he" rather than "she"? Similarly for roles at home. What illustrations are used in preaching, and what messages do they give off about gender roles?

These sorts of examples unpick the assumptions we make, the culture we have and what will be communicated as a result. It is very helpful for upfront leaders, especially those preaching regularly, to get feedback on this as we are often blind to own tendencies and deaf to our own voices.

EMBRACING COMPLEMENTARIANISM

This chapter has laid out what we think are some key first steps for how complementarianism can begin to be embraced more in your church. If you are an elder with responsibility for a congregation, it may sound like a daunting amount of hard work! But we want to finish by encouraging you that the hard work is worth it. It's our hope and prayer that by engaging in this process, you will lead your flock into greater clarity, conviction, confidence and joy about complementarianism in the months and years ahead—for the good of Christ's people and to the glory of God.

REFLECTION QUESTIONS
For a group
1. What position do we hold on complementarianism?
2. What areas need to be clarified?
3. How have we communicated this to our church? Does more need to be done?
4. What steps might we take on pursuing this in practice?
5. What ongoing messaging might we send about the role of men and women?

Appendix 1
Can Only Elders Preach?

We've approached the discussion about complementarianism in practice by looking at the role of elders, and in chapter 5 we argued that this role should be reserved for qualified men. In the "mapping exercise" outlined in chapter 8, we said that asking how much something qualifies as an "elder" role is, then, a key question.

So far, so good. But that raises a question about preaching: if preaching fulfils an "elder role", from which women are excluded, should only elders preach? The reason why this gets raised is that many churches have men preach who are not elders. Should they stop? And if they shouldn't, might women preach occasionally as well, on the same basis as those men?

We should back up here to clarify one issue: what do we mean by preaching? It's important to recognise that some of our standard forms of Bible teaching in churches today—such as a 30-minute monologue delivered by one person—might not have been the standard in 1st-century churches. The word translated "preach" usually means "exhort" or "declare", without specifying how exactly it is be done. Certainly, we know that some people gave monologues in the early church (for example, Acts 2:14-36), but we don't know if that was the usual form that teaching took week by week.

So our argument works more from the dynamics in play: if someone preaches in the modern form, what is happening? It is an uncontested declaration of God's truth to a congregation, usually guiding the way its members will live together. So, should only elders do that?

First, we'd say that elders should be the usual people to preach because preaching is a key way in which they shepherd the church. Anyone who speaks in that way with any regularity becomes a de facto elder in that congregation. They are exercising a teaching authority and guiding the life of the church—which is key to the role of elder.

But what about someone just speaking occasionally, either as a guest from elsewhere or from within the congregation? Are they being given permission to speak by the elders and so speaking "under" their authority? If so, could not a woman do the same on occasion? Some complementarian churches do operate that way; others only have extra speakers who are male; others limit all their preaching to those who are elders.

The question is this: is a restriction on women preaching tied to the office of elder (and so, by extension, to sex) or to sex itself?

This is where we need to go back to the reason given for the limitation in 1 Timothy 2 ("I do not permit a woman to teach or to assume authority over a man; she must be quiet," verse 12). Paul bases his restriction on the order of creation (v 13). In doing so, he is showing that there is something in how God wants men and women to relate, which is seen in women not exercising this teaching function over men. That way of relating will be seen in women not being elders but also in women not acting in an "elder-like" way towards men. So the restriction is tied to sex first and then to the office of elder secondarily. That is why many churches are then happy to have a male non-elder preach occasionally; such preachers are contributing in an "elder-like" way and so should be male, but are being co-opted by the elders for their contribution.

We recognise some complementarians disagree on that.

Some allow occasional female speakers, either because of a different view of preaching or because of a different understanding of how someone can speak under the authority of the elders. Our conclusion, though, is that elders should be the regular preachers of a congregation and that while other people may preach occasionally, these should also be male.

This also raises another question in some settings: who are the elders? In some churches that is very clear because the elders are a recognised group; they are often elected by the congregation and meet regularly to discuss the leadership of the church, so there's no ambiguity as to who they are. In such a situation, it is not that every elder must then preach regularly. Most elderships would have a variety of giftings represented, and while every elder should teach in some way, that need not be by preaching (although it's worth reflecting in those situations on how "non-preaching" elders might exercise their leadership in other ways or feed into the regular preaching).

In other churches, though, it is less clear who the elders are. There may be a minister or vicar who is clearly an "elder". There is sometimes an assistant minister (or curate) who is usually also an elder, although sometimes they might be relatively young and so are not seen in this way. In some churches there are other positions, such as church wardens and others. We mentioned in our "mapping exercise" that you need to consider whether these are "elder" positions or not.

All of this is relevant to being clear on who might preach. Remember that anyone preaching regularly is functionally acting as an elder, whether they have that title or not. Having the standard positions of "elders" and "deacons" that we've seen in the Bible makes all this much clearer in church life. Where churches have other structures, they should try to be clear on who the elders are; they are the group the congregation should submit to, who should be responsible for the overall teaching of the church, and so those who preach regularly.

Appendix 2
Common Grey Areas

Some of the common questions asked about what women can do in the life of a church are...

- can they lead services?
- can they lead singing/worship within services?
- can they lead a mixed-sex Bible study?
- can they lead a mixed-sex youth group?

In the mapping exercise described in chapter 8, we said that a key question is to what extent something qualifies as an "elder" role. That is, how much does it exercise the teaching/authority combination we described from 1 Timothy 2? To put it another way, and to again borrow Andrew Wilson's helpful terminology, we have distinguished between the "big-T Teaching" of the elders and the "little-t teaching" of everyone in the congregation.

Of course, if you disagree with that distinction in types of teaching as described in the New Testament, you might simply say that women cannot teach any men in any context. That will almost certainly mean that the answer to all the questions above is "No" because some level of teaching is often involved in each. If, however, you agree with that distinction, then you will expect women to be teaching in some ways and not in others, and the question becomes "Is this area big-T or little-t teaching?" Many of these instances will probably feel like grey areas, although some might be clearer than others.

Along with that approach to restriction, we must include the contributions that we know women played in New Testament church life that we described in chapter 7 on ministry: women prayed and prophesied in public, made significant financial contributions and took part in the "one-another commands" addressed to all believers. In other words, Scripture gives us both a caution, because of God's limitation of some roles to men, and an encouragement, because of wanting the right enriching contribution of women.

In answering the question "What type of teaching does this role entail?" it is key that we ask what is actually happening in each of the areas listed. We often know what we mean by a particular role in church life—we talk about someone "leading" a service, for example—but we've rarely examined it in any detail. And that means we've not asked whether the person is acting as an elder in what they are doing or what sort of teaching/authority is being exercised in this role. It may be that you don't think any of the examples above involve teaching with elder-type authority, and so you are happy for women to do all of them. That is basically Graham's position. For others, it might depend on exactly what is happening and how it is done, and this is where different people will probably have differing opinions (as Graham and Jane have).

For example, some Bible-study leading is very much about enabling others to see what it is in a passage, while other forms are much more directive and didactic. That might make a difference to your judgement or it might not—you might be happy with a women doing either. Remember that other relational dynamics are in play as well: the nature of the group, its regularity, age differential, and so on. This is where we need to admit that some things are a judgement call and we will probably land in different positions.

To take another example, what is happening in leading a worship service? This usually involves reading Scripture, leading in prayer and introducing songs. That can, of course, have a teaching element, but you might think that it is all of the little-t variety and so involve women in doing that. Meanwhile, others think of leading services as an eldership task. Sometimes that's because they think there is more authoritative teaching happening, akin to preaching. In other cases, it's because of a view of ordained ministry, with leading the corporate gathering being the role of the ordained leaders of the church. That is often especially the case when it comes to conducting the sacraments of the Lord's Supper and baptism.

All of this means you need to be clear on the key convictions we outlined in chapter 8: what different levels of teaching and leadership you think operate in the church and which women can do. Then you need to reflect on these grey areas of ministry and ask what is happening in each of them. As we've said before, this is an exercise primarily for the church's leaders, but it is important to include others in it. If, for example, you have different people leading services, what do they think they are doing? What teaching do they think they are exercising? Getting everyone on the same page is key.

Once you have decided on these grey areas, make sure to be clear and positive in articulating your position. One of the worst outcomes of a process like this is when women are asked to lead in some new areas but are given the impression that it is a reluctant concession, or even that they may be doing something wrong in accepting the invitation. That's a horribly awkward position to be placed in, and it's the responsibility of the leaders to avoid that happening. Decide where you land and then embrace your decisions!

Appendix 3
Women on Staff Teams

Having women on your staff team can help your local church achieve its mission. If we believe that God has created men and women to complement each other, then we recognise that a male brings something to a relationship/ ministry that a female cannot, and a female brings something that a male cannot. So, where possible, it can be helpful to have both men and women on church staff teams.

Maybe you desire to have a woman on staff but do not see how this is possible financially. Women (just like men) on staff teams could be paid full-time or part-time by the church (as long as, in the case of the latter, the scope of their role is adjusted accordingly). They may also raise their own funds or part of their own funds (depending on the church). For some women, their personal circumstances may allow them to serve voluntarily. This may be particularly possible for some older married women. Not all women want full-time paid ministry positions. Some want part-time jobs because of the other responsibilities they have in life: for example, looking after young children or elderly parents. Or they might choose, for a variety of reasons, to work part-time in a secular job alongside a ministry role. Some churches find that they have to employ a woman initially on a part-time basis, but they plan the budget so that her position will gradually increase to full-time over, say, five years.

A woman's life situation and circumstances typically change more than a man's, with marriage and motherhood most often bringing about those changes. Rather than this working against having women on church staff teams, these changes can open up different possibilities and can help churches think outside the box and employ more women on their staff teams. For instance, those on staff teams could encourage some women to not go back to their secular employment but instead work for the church, if those women are in a situation to be able to do that. A number of women would love to work for their church, but they would never initiate a conversation with their pastor about it.

All that said, it is nonetheless important—both ethically and legally—that there is parity in rates of pay between men and women on a staff team, in line with their experience and levels of responsibility. "The worker deserves his wages" (1 Timothy 5:18)—and that extends to female workers too.

Depending on her gifting and what the church needs, there are numerous ministries a woman on staff may do: for example, ministry to women, seniors, students, youth or children; engaging in evangelism; training congregation members. Some churches divide ministries into broad areas such as "evangelism", "discipleship", "worship", "maturity", and so on. If so, a woman might lead or co-lead with a man on one of these areas.

Any woman a church employs needs to be godly and well-thought-out theologically. This might be someone from within your own congregation or someone from outside. Ideally, she would have some theological training, although, as when hiring a man, exactly what is suitable will depend on the role envisaged. If a woman is going to be teaching the Bible in some way and doesn't have any formal training, that is something it may well be good to offer as part of her role. View this as a valuable kingdom investment. Formal training should help further develop her biblical, theological and ministry thinking, and, therefore, she will be more confident as a ministry leader. And it's important that she is thought of and acts as a Christian leader. Having a woman who thinks theologically on your staff means she can not only think wisely about the ministries she is responsible for but also contribute meaningfully to staff discussions about other ministries across the church.

Whatever ministry a female staff member is responsible for, ideally she will also be seeking to raise up others in the congregation to do the ministry, or some of the ministry, that she does. For example, a female worker who is responsible for women's ministry helps women in the congregation become more confident in ministries such as one-to-one Bible reading, leading Bible-study groups and evangelism. This is because she acknowledges and rejoices in the gifts of the congregation and wants to best use them to build Christ's church. She is not threatened by other people's gifts. She will probably see female church members doing ministry in situations that male staff will not (in, say, single-sex Bible studies), and she gets to know these women in ways the male staff cannot. She can therefore help raise up more workers and multiply the ministries that women are involved in. Having a woman on staff means that someone has been set apart and has time to do this type of training and equipping, and that should bear great fruit.

Having a staff of both men and women is of great benefit to the church more broadly, not just in the area of ministry for which a female staff member is responsible. For example, there might be a difficult pastoral situation where a male staff member brings in a female colleague, or vice versa. But it is also beneficial in the normal run of weekly staff meetings: for example, when giving feedback on sermons and services, planning preaching programmes or devising

GRAHAM BEYNON AND JANE TOOHER

ministry training for church members. It means there are more people on staff who have perhaps closer relationships with a greater breadth of the congregation. Christian men and women are co-workers in Christ, and having a healthy and happy mixed-sex church staff team can be an excellent way to express this, with great ripple effects in the rest of the church. It's worth being aware, however, that many women find that if they're the only woman in a meeting, it can be harder to speak up. Male staff members need to create an environment where the woman on staff knows that her ideas are just as welcome as anyone else's.

Good management and care of a staff team is key. It is important to be clear on to whom a female staff member is answerable—to have clearly articulated line management. A female staff member (like any assistant, male or female) needs regular meetings with her senior pastor to help facilitate good communication and care. Ideally there will also be weekly staff meetings with all of the senior staff. But in addition to this, there needs to be organised one-to-one meetings when both the senior pastor and the female staff member can bring up issues more specific to her. And, as for any staff member, if a person has issues with their immediate boss, there needs to be someone else they can bring issues to. Who this person/people will be will vary depending on your governance structures. But what's important is that each staff member is clear on who it is.

Along with meeting with their (male) boss, some women find it helpful to have an appointed mature female member of the congregation that they regularly meet with; others find it more helpful when such a woman is from a different church. And an increasing number of staff, both male and female, are choosing to meet semi-regularly with someone who has been trained in pastoral supervision. Some elders have decided that each staff member needs to have professional supervision and that the church will pay for it.

Although vocational ministry is different to a non-vocational job in many ways, it can be helpful if the staff member has a job description. This is good not just for the staff member but also for the elders. It brings clarity to her role, and it is something that either party can use as a reference point (although it may need tweaking over time as circumstances change). Along with a job description, it is helpful to be explicit about what other benefits are included in her employment package, such as a book allowance, study leave provision, pension contributions, holiday entitlement, and so on. Again, parity with male staff members in these areas is important. Including benefits such as these communicates that a church values its female staff member and wants her to keep growing in the gifts God has given her as a Christian leader.

Appendix 4
Writing a Position Paper

For elders / staff members writing a position paper on complementarianism, following this structure may be of help.

INTRODUCTION
In your introductory paragraph, state what your paper will do: e.g. "This paper will look at the biblical foundation for the ministries of men and women and how they apply to [insert the name of your church]". It is also helpful to include a sentence about God's word since your argument will be based on the Bible: e.g. "The Bible is God's good and infallible word and his authority for how we live and minister together as men and women". State who is/are the author(s) of the paper.

SELECT BIBLICAL PASSAGES
Introduce the pertinent biblical passages and briefly explain what they mean. These are likely to include passages that help explain theologically what it means to be a man and a woman, e.g. Genesis 1 – 3; Ephesians 5:21-33; passages that show how each one of us is gifted to serve the church, e.g. Romans 12:3-8; 1 Corinthians 12; and those that speak of order and restrictions in the gathered assembly, e.g. 1 Corinthians 11:2-16; 14; 1 Timothy 2 – 3. It is also worth noting the breadth of ministries that we see men and women contribute to in the New Testament, particularly in Jesus' and Paul's ministries,

and which ones are applicable to us today. This helps us see that the Pauline restrictions on non-elder men and on women are very few compared to the numerous ministry possibilities that may be open to a specific individual.

APPLICATION TO YOUR CHURCH
Explain how the above applies to your church: its governance, Sunday services and mid-week ministries. Be clear about the ministries you want different people to be serving in. Include examples of ministries you want men and women doing together and whether there are any which you think it is good to have as single-sex ministries. Areas to explicitly cover may include...

- for your church governance: e.g. elders, deacons, staff, parish council, churchwardens, trustees, council, external advisors.
- for Sunday services: e.g. preaching, leading services, Bible reading, leading in prayers, leading singing, testimony spots upfront, children's/family talks.
- for mid-week ministries: e.g. leading Bible-study groups, involvement in pastoral care/visitation teams, leading youth ministry, leading children's ministry.

CONCLUSION
Include how thankful you are for God's good design and purpose in having men and women minister together and underlines how we complement each other to serve Christ's church. It is probably helpful to include something that makes clear that you are more than happy to keep talking about this topic and that you are always learning: e.g. "Please come and speak to me about any ministry ideas, suggestions, questions or concerns you may have." This can also help people have more ownership of the paper, which is paramount if complementarianism is to be truly embraced by the congregation and not just the authors of the paper.

Endnotes

1 Michelle Lee-Barnewall, *Neither Complementarian Nor Egalitarian: A Kingdom Corrective to the Evangelical Gender Debate* (Baker, 2016), p 11-13.

2 For this term and the background on this cultural shift see Carl R. Trueman, *The Rise and Triumph of the Modern Self: Cultural Amnesia, Expressive Individualism, and the Road to Sexual Revolution* (Crossway [US], 2020).

3 As one example, see Paul T. Costa Jr., Antonio Terracciano, and Robert R. McCrae, "Gender Differences in Personality Traits across Cultures: Robust and Surprising Findings", *Journal of Personality and Social Psychology,* 8 (2001): p 322–331. See also a summary by Steven Pinker, *The Blank Slate,* chapter 18.

4 This has been particularly noted in Scandinavian countries, which have a strong push towards social equality, and has been called the "Nordic Gender Equality Paradox". See for example, "BHATIA: Sweden Hasn't Achieved Gender Equality", The Daily Free Press, https://dailyfreepress.com/2017/02/23/bhatia-sweden-hasnt-achieved-gender-equality/ (accessed 7 Apr. 2021).

5 Steven Pinker, *The Blank Slate,* p 343.

6 World Female Imprisonment List, https://www.prisonstudies.org/sites/default/files/resources/downloads/world_female_prison_4th_edn_v4_web.pdf (accessed 21 April 22).

7 Simone de Beauvoir, *The Second Sex,* trans. H. M. Parshley (London: Vintage Books, 1997), p 295.

8 For example, Ashley McGuire, *Sex Scandal: The Drive to*

Abolish Male and Female (Regnery Publishing, 2017).

9 Alastair Roberts, "Man and Woman in Creation (Genesis 1 and 2)", *9 Marks Journal Complementarianism: A Moment of Reckoning* (December 2019), p 39.

10 Pinker, *The Blank Slate,* p 350–51.

11 https://www.desiringgod.org/interviews/should-women-be-police-officers (accessed 24 Mar. 2022).

12 https://www.reformation21.org/mos/housewife-theologian/john-pipers-advice-for-women-in-the-workforce (accessed 24 Mar. 2022)

13 https://www.reformation21.org/mos/postcards-from-palookaville/an-accidental-feminist (accessed 24 Mar. 2022)

14 That is where men were assumed to be superior and so should hold power over all women.

15 Rachel Green Miller, *Beyond Authority and Submission: Women and Men in Marriage, Church, and Society* (P&R, 2019), p 14.

16 Dorothy L. Sayers, *Are Women Human? Astute and Witty Essays on the Role of Women in Society* (Eerdmans, 2005), p 53.

17 Claire Smith, *God's Good Design: What the Bible Really Says about Men and Women* (Matthias Media, 2019) p 47.

18 These are my summary taken from Alastair Roberts, "Man and Woman in Creation (Genesis 1 and 2)", *9 Marks Journal,* December 2019.

19 See for example Sam A. Andreades, *EnGendered: God's Gift of Gender Difference in Relationship* (Weaver Book Company, 2015).

20 Sarah Sumner, *Men and Women in the Church* (IVP [US], 2003), p 28.

21 Sumner, *Men and Women in the Church*, p 42-48.

22 Wyatt Edward Gates, "How Men Constantly and Casually Drive Women out of the Workplace", Medium,

12 July 2018, https://medium.com/@wyattegates/how-men-constantly-and-casually-drive-women-out-of-the-workplace-6d66d61d3adc (accessed 21 Apr. 2022).

23 Jen Wilkin, "3 Female Ghosts That Haunt the Church", The Gospel Coalition, https://www.thegospelcoalition.org/article/3-female-ghosts-that-haunt-the-church/ (accessed 24 Mar. 2022).

24 Sumner, *Men and Women in the Church,* p 78.

25 Andreades, *EnGendered,* p 49.

26 Andreades, *EnGendered*, p 61, 65.

27 Gary L. Welton, "My Human Identity Transcends Gender", The Institute for Faith and Freedom (blog), 20 July 2017, https://www.faithandfreedom.com/my-human-identity-transcends-gender/(accessed 29 Mar. 2022).

28 Michael Bird, "Imitation of Christ vs. Gender Roles (Updated)", Euangelion (blog), 24 Mar. 2020, https://www.patheos.com/blogs/euangelion/2020/03/imitation-of-christ-vs-gender-roles/(accessed 29 Mar. 2022).

29 Brandon O'Brien, "How Manly Is Jesus?", ChristianityToday.com, https://www.christianitytoday.com/ct/2008/april/27.48.html (accessed 13 May 2020).

30 Alastair Roberts, "Man and Woman in Creation (Genesis 1 and 2)". Emphasis original.

31 Jonathan Leeman, "Biblical Manhood and Womanhood—Or Christlikeness?", *9Marks*, https://www.9marks.org/article/biblical-manhood-and-womanhood-or-christlikeness/(accessed 29 Mar. 2022).

32 Leeman, as above.

33 Sayers, *Are Women Human?*, p 68-69.

34 Douglas Murray, *The Madness of Crowds: Gender, Race and Identity* (Bloomsbury Continuum, 2019), p 174-83.

35 For a proponent of this view, see John G. Stackhouse Jnr., *Partners in Christ: A Conservative Case for Egalitarianism*

(IVP Academic, 2015).

36 See Lionel Windsor, "The Work of Ministry in Ephesians 4:12" in *Tend My Sheep: The Word of God and Pastoral Ministry* (ed. Keith Condie), (Latimer Publications, 2016).

37 Claire Smith, *God's Good Design,* p 35.

38 A comprehensive text is Andreas J. Köstenberger and Thomas R. Schreiner, eds., *Women in the Church: An Interpretation and Application of 1 Timothy 2:9-15* (Crossway, 2016).

39 Andrew Wilson, 'Teaching with a Little "t" and a Big "T"', https://thinktheology.co.uk/blog/article/teaching-with-a-little-t-and-a-big-t (accessed 29 Mar. 2022).

40 For a helpful resource on 1 Timothy 2:8-15 see Claire Smith, *God's Good Design.*

41 For more on 1 Corinthians 11:2-16, see Danny Rurlander, "1 Corinthians 11:2-16", https://paa.moore.edu.au/resources/1-corinthians-112-16-by-danny-rurlander-02-02-15/ (accessed 29 Mar. 2022); Claire Smith, as above.

42 See Danny Rurlander, as above. For more on 1 Corinthians 14 see, Claire Smith, as above.

43 For example Titus is told to appoint elders but not deacons (Titus 1:5).

44 See Kevin DeYoung, *Men and Women in the Church: A Short, Biblical, Practical Introduction* (Crossway, 2021), p 92-93.

45 Anglican, Presbyterian and Baptist denominations often have their own specific definitions.

46 Jonathan Leeman, "Essential and Indispensable: Women and the Mission of the Church", *9 Marks Journal* (Dec 2019), p 33.

47 Jen Wilkin, "The Complementarian Woman: Permitted or Pursued?", https://www.thegospelcoalition.org/article/the-complementarian-woman-permitted-or-pursued/

(accessed 21 Apr. 2022).

48 Lionel Windsor, "Principles of complementarian ministry", http://www.lionelwindsor.net/2017/09/28/principles-complementarian-ministry/ (accessed 21 Apr. 2022).
49 For example, Andrew Wilson, "Women Preachers: A Response to John Piper," https://thinktheology.co.uk/blog/article/women_preachers_a_response_to_john_piper (accessed 26 May 2022).

BIBLICAL | RELEVANT | ACCESSIBLE

At The Good Book Company, we are dedicated to helping Christians and local churches grow. We believe that God's growth process always starts with hearing clearly what he has said to us through his timeless word—the Bible.

Ever since we opened our doors in 1991, we have been striving to produce Bible-based resources that bring glory to God. We have grown to become an international provider of user-friendly resources to the Christian community, with believers of all backgrounds and denominations using our books, Bible studies, devotionals, evangelistic resources, and DVD-based courses.

We want to equip ordinary Christians to live for Christ day by day, and churches to grow in their knowledge of God, their love for one another, and the effectiveness of their outreach.

Call us for a discussion of your needs or visit one of our local websites for more information on the resources and services we provide.

Your friends at The Good Book Company

thegoodbook.com | thegoodbook.co.uk
thegoodbook.com.au | thegoodbook.co.nz
thegoodbook.co.in